The Assignment

**SHE MUST
NOT FULFILL
HER DESTINY**

Helen Swift

ACW PRESS
Phoenix, Arizona 85013

The Assignment
Copyright ©2000 Helen Swift

Cover design by Pine Hill Graphics
Interior design by Pine Hill Graphics

Packaged by ACW Press
5501 N. 7th Ave., #502
Phoenix, Arizona 85013
www.acwpress.com
The views expressed or implied in this work do not necessarily reflect those of ACW Press. Ultimate design, content, and editorial accuracy of this work is the responsibility of the author(s).

Printed in the United States of America by Bethany Press International, Bloomington, Minnesota 55438.

ISBN 1-892525-26-7

Acknowledgements

This book would not have been possible without the love and patience of my sons: Marquis, Joseph and Jeremy. Thank you for your unselfish natures in sharing me with so many. Words cannot express how much all three of you mean to me, but I am confident that you know that I love you and am honored to be your mother.

Special thanks to my friend, my confidante, and spiritual sister Shirley. You are a remarkable person. Painful circumstances brought us closer, and the love of God has healed our wounds. I love you Shirley. To Laura my faithful listening ear. The Bible says, "A friend loves at all times." It was chance that made us cousins, but choice that made us friends. Thank you cousin. To my "big sister" Loretta. Thank you for believing in me, encouraging me and giving me the sense of family that I so desperately needed. We have come such a long way in our relationship. Mamma would be so proud of you.

To all of my spiritual family at the House of Refuge. God brought me over 1500 miles to unite me with you because he knew you would pray me through to victory. You have loved me, blessed me, and welcomed me into a foreign land with open arms. You know this book would not have been possible without all of your support.

I didn't forget you Sadie. You have been my mirror. When I look into your eyes and see the excitement and love, you remind me that I have been chosen by God for a special work. When I listen to your voice, I feel hope and assurance that the ministry that God has ordained for me "surely" will come to pass.

To Lorraine, the matriarch of our family. My mother (your

cousin and friend) passed a mantle on to you to take care of us; Loretta, Annette and me. You have never wavered in your support and love, and I know that I can always depend on you. I love you.

To the Body of Believers who have prayed for me, wept for me and pulled me through, I am eternally grateful for your not giving up on me when the battles were raging. Our God is an awesome God.

Contents

Chapter Three:
Free at Last

Chapter One

In the Beginning

In the Beginning

The Lord woke me up last year and told me to write a book. Actually, he told me that I would write several books. He even gave me the titles. Of course, like most people I was waiting for this divine timing. I thought that all of my trials must be completed before I began. I realize now that was foolish thinking, coupled with tons of fear. Yes, I know fear is not from God so don't bother quoting me scriptures. After I share my journey perhaps you will understand my years of hesitation. So much has occurred in my life over the past twelve years. I asked the Lord where to begin. The Father simply told me to start at the beginning.

Let me prepare you. I have learned through my process to be honest and real. I will try not to get too graphic. With things that may seem a bit offensive, however, I will share only what I know to be relevant. I grew up with the truth being covered up by adults and I was left to figure out too many things on my own.

I grew up in a traditional Baptist church. I don't remember a time when I did not go to church and all of the functions. I finished high school and went to college. I made a lot of mistakes, but I graduated and returned to my hometown in 1977. At that time, the Lord had visited the youth of our church and had filled several of them with the Holy Ghost. Needless to say the adults were not at all happy. Nevertheless, the youth minister, Andrea Jones, began

9

to tell me about the baptism of the Holy Ghost. I had never heard of it but was desperate to rid myself of inner turmoil. Praise God when I received the baptism of the Holy Ghost, there was no stopping me. At least, I thought not. One evening shortly thereafter, the youth were gathered in a room by the pastor and we were forbidden to speak in tongues. Maybe I should clarify that. He forbade *Them* because I was then twenty-one years old and no longer had to remain in the family church. As I recall, only a couple of us left. My family was not at all pleased, but what could they do, I so desperately needed the Holy Ghost.

I was married at age twenty-two. I married one of the youth in that group and I mean just that, I married one of the YOUTH. I had finished college and he was just finishing high school. It was strange because although there was a lot of lust involved in the beginning, I knew that the Lord had said that he was to be my husband. For once in my life, I was going against the norm (which was not at all my character). I needed the Holy Spirit. Let's face it, either I was definitely hearing from God or I wasn't. The Lord even told me that my first child was a boy and to name him Marquis. Back then, they weren't doing ultrasounds (and to this day I still can't read one) so when I had my son, I knew that it had been God speaking to me.

The Lord soon spoke to my husband and told him that he was going to preach. I was so blessed because all I ever truly wanted in my life was to be married, have children and go to church. I never really had a career goal in my heart other than to do something for God and be married. My husband's age only bothered me when others had a problem with it. I had so much respect for him. To me, he stood taller than any man that I knew. He seemed so strong and I felt so safe. I had a lot of childhood scars and I needed some strength. Now I had it. I was married, we had a son, and we were going to church.

As we began to study the Word, my vision broadened. My husband began to preach and I believed in him, but we didn't have much of a foundation. When we married, we lived in Oklahoma City for a while, but after about a year, I heard the Lord tell us to go back home and we returned to our hometown. At this time, the Lord sent a powerful man of God in to our lives—Pastor Marvin Boyd—to start a church. We sat under his teaching and we were spellbound. It was like bread from heaven. If the church door was open, we were there. That was in 1980 and to this day that foundation is still within my heart. Pastor Boyd made the scriptures come alive in me. He often taught on the gifts of the Spirit and as I studied alongside other precious saints, I decided which gift I would seek God for. I saw others operating in several of the gifts, but I wanted the gift of discerning of spirits. Now, much to my embarrassment, I thought that to operate in that gift all I had to do was walk by someone and I would know what demon they had. I'm being painfully honest here. I really believed that was how it would operate, or at least, that is the way I wanted it to operate. I did not understand that I would literally have to go to the bowels of hell and back, several times, to truly operate in this precious gift.

Pastor Boyd picked up where the previous young minister had left off. He helped us to understand exactly what the Holy Ghost was. My husband and I lived for church. The transformation in our lives was very obvious. The Power of God was upon us so strongly that soon afterwards, our friends and family members became cautious about cursing around us. I know they couldn't quite figure out the drastic change in us, but it didn't matter to us because we knew we were right where we should be and it seemed as if we were growing by leaps and bounds. The church had revivals, shut-in's, and evangelistic services every Friday night as well as Sunday morning and evening services. People from all denominations would come to fellowship with us on evangelistic nights. The Lord began to give us clear direction about our future and our destiny. My husband had such a strong desire to preach the gospel and I had that same burning within my heart. I began my ministry by simply testifying. It seemed as if the anointing of the Holy Ghost would fall on me every time I would testify. I know I was still a babe in the Lord, but the Word was alive and we searched the scriptures daily.

As my husband's father had died when he was very young, and he deeply desired the relationship of a father, Pastor Boyd took my husband under his wing. Although he was a fairly young man himself, he gave my husband the love, guidance, support, and direction he so deeply desired. I know that he recognized the strength in my husband as I did. At that time, I often struggled with many fears, however my husband seemed fearless. I recall one summer evening, while we were walking home from church, a Doberman pincher began to chase us. It was a neighbors' dog and we knew he was ferocious. My husband was carrying our oldest son and holding my hand as the dog approached us. I was pregnant with our second son at the time, but I was very prepared to break out into a sprint. To say that I was afraid is an understatement. With the dog directly at our backs my husband gripped my hand tightly and calmly said, "Just keep walking." I could see our infant in his arms looking down at the dog. He was afraid also. Naturally, I wanted to scream, but my husband continued to calmly say, "Just keep walking and don't look back." At one point the dog just stopped. I suppose at that moment my husband grew taller to me. My God, what a blessing he was to me.

The Brotherhood and Sisterhood organizations in the church gave us the relationships we longed for with our natural families.

We were somewhat distanced from our natural family because of our (as they put it) newfound religion. We wanted our families to experience what we had, but they were skeptical and critical. So, we spent quite a bit of time with our *new* family. I will admit, however, that we probably crossed over a "wee bit" into the self-righteous realm. God had to show us ourselves many times and teach us to walk in love. I suppose most babes in the Lord have the same struggle at one point. We didn't mind the chastisement of the Lord. We were just happy to be in the family of God. Remember, I grew up in a church that didn't worship like this. I knew a lot of Bible stories, but I had not accepted Jesus back then. All I had done was to join the church. I said, "I believe in God and I want to be baptized." That was it. I was baptized, joined the choir, and said what everyone else said. That's how I knew what to say.

I didn't grow up around a lot of children like my husband did. I had a sister who was one year older than myself, and a brother who was thirteen years younger who died of TaySachs disease when I was nineteen. My older brother and sister were in college when I was in elementary school so, at home it was just my sister and me. My husband, on the other hand, was one of ten siblings so he loved children like no one I had ever met. My mother sometimes said he was a *big kid* himself. They had a really good relationship. I must admit it was better than my own relationship with my mother. As I reflect on their relationship I understand their bond now. She grew up without a mother and he grew up without a father. In a silent kind of way, they somehow understood each other.

Having grown up with so many siblings, I suppose my husband understood certain behaviors in children that were totally foreign to me. I remember one evening, he had gone to visit one of the brothers of the church when suddenly my twelve-month-old infant son fell to the floor screaming in pain. I panicked. I didn't know what to do. He screamed and screamed in pain and I was helpless. He couldn't really talk yet, so he couldn't tell me what was wrong. I prayed and prayed for him but it didn't help. I grabbed the phone and called my husband. I was frustrated because he didn't seem alarmed. It seemed as if he didn't care as he just said, okay. A few days later it happened again. This time he was home and I ran to get him, but he didn't react to my panic. He calmly came into the room, picked up our son, tapped his legs and told him to knock it off. To my amazement our son's pain left him. He was healed! Well, needless to say I had witnessed my first two real tantrums. I had never seen one before and, to my further amazement, he never had another one.

Our new church family began to grow but my husband was somehow hurt by one of the evangelists. To this day, I don't know what happened. I'm not even sure which evangelist caused the damage. I'm pretty sure the evangelist didn't know that my husband was hurt. My husband never gave me any details. He was never one to talk negatively about anyone, so he kept it buried deep within. Then he was laid off from work and had a difficult time obtaining employment. He looked daily, sought God and, it seemed, found no answer. I was pregnant, he was unemployed and we couldn't pay our bills. Friends encouraged us to file for bankruptcy and we did. We were young and didn't know any better. At that time, our emotions overrode the voice of God. Isn't it amazing when we discover how little faith we have when our faith is tried? We got immediate relief from our creditors, but we didn't know that there would be a price to pay for that decision later.

We continued to pray for employment, and soon the Power Company in our hometown called my husband in. It was a very well-paying job and it came just in time as on my husband's fifth day of work I went into labor. We were not only blessed with another son, but he was born on my husband's birthday.

Through a series of events, my husband and I left that church. I'm not entirely sure if we missed hearing God or not. We thought we heard God say that it was time to leave. A short time later, the Pastor and his family relocated. Today, they have a very strong ministry in Denver and I will forever thank God for the foundation that he allowed to be so carefully laid.

We were led to a church that was out of our neighborhood. I realize now that the Lord was using that church to prepare me for where I am now. It was another church on the move and the pastors were fireballs for the Lord. The congregation was predominantly Caucasian and we were welcomed with opened arms. We were so blessed and my husband and I were ordained together. All of my immediate family came to the ordination ceremony. It was a bit of a surprise since they were still in the family church, which denied the Power of God. I remember the look in my mother's eyes as she embraced me. I had never seen so much hope in her eyes before. It was as if she knew, deep in her heart, that the Lord was going to use us far beyond anything even she could comprehend. She held me so tight, even though my family was never really affectionate. My parents, siblings and I had never really hugged one another.

My husband and I talked much about the Lord. Soon after the ordination he said to me, "I don't want to be an ordinary preacher, I want to be a deliverer." I did also, but I didn't realize then that it wouldn't come without a price!

To the Country

My family and I moved into a house in the country and that was when this new journey began. It was the house of a cousin of mine who had gotten sick. My cousin's house had been there all of my life. I remember going there when I was a little girl when my cousin had a couple other young girls there from the church. She had us all sitting in a circle on the floor while she read our palms. I was afraid and I didn't want her to read my palm, but my father told me to sit down and let her. He said there was no harm in it. He also told me that she used to read his palm a lot. I felt trapped. Years later I was renting the same house.

My husband never wanted me to work and that was fine with me. You see, he wanted to take care of us and I wanted to be taken care of. Maybe I put my husband on a pedestal, maybe I didn't, who knows? What I do know is that I loved him and he was good to our sons and me. I never struggled with being a submissive wife because he was easy to submit to. At this particular time we didn't have a car. My husband would walk to work and walk home. When he didn't get a ride, he never complained. Never. With each passing day it seemed as if the presence of God was always around. We were young in age, and young in the Lord, but we knew what we wanted. We fasted and prayed together. We had experienced God moving in our lives in so many ways, but I still hungered for the gift of discerning of spirits.

In my zeal, I was missing something really important about the gift of discerning of spirits. I knew something about demons, I knew that I was tormented for most of my childhood and I knew from the Bible about the signs that follow the believers. What I didn't know about was warfare. Real warfare. Even today, I know that the Body of Christ is truly lacking in real spiritual warfare. I, and many other people that I have come into contact with since my journey into darkness, have been deeply hurt by the Body of Christ. No, not deliberately, but truly out of ignorance. Many pastors, evangelists, teachers, and saints have told me many things in reference to my warfare that were not truly God. Nothing worked and I was always made to feel as if there was something I wasn't doing right. Kind of like Job. Oh, now I'm not comparing myself to Job, but remember his friends who believed his calamity was due to sin in his life?

I enjoyed my life then. I had my sons, and my husband had a good job. We didn't have much money, but I was happy and my children were also. My immediate family thought I was crazy for not working since I had a college degree and was simply living in the country with my three sons and my husband. I didn't care, though. At least I knew we had God and we were happy.

Things began to change, but not enough for me to notice initially. Although my husband was still good to me, he started slipping away. After a while, I would get up at night to find him in front of the television. I didn't have a problem with him watching the television, but I had a problem with what he was watching. He was always engrossed in Dr. Ruth or some sex-related program. When I would ask him to come to bed, or ask why he was watching those shows, he always had the same reply: "You can learn a lot of stuff."

Strange things began to happen after a few months. My children seemed to be having what we thought were nightmares. However, the nightmares were always the same ones. Our youngest son would always see a dark creature wearing really bright colors. He described the creature as being so dark that it looked burned. This creature would always stare at him for long periods of time. It wore really nice sneakers and would have another pair in his hand for my son. The strange thing is, on different occasions my other son would see and describe the same creature. Also, my oldest son said that a large cobra snake would appear in the middle of the night. It would spread its fangs and they would stare at one another. Both sons said that whenever they would call out for their father, the creature would run away and when he left, it would come back. My oldest son told me years later that at one point he became tired of calling his father, so one night he took a swing at the snake. He said his hand went right through it. It never came back.

I didn't know, then, that demons have territorial rights. I didn't realize that the ground was cursed because of the activities that had transpired over the years in my house. I didn't know to anoint the house and pray over the ground. I did know to anoint my children and I did that frequently. I really thank God for that knowledge.

Another Son

We remained committed to God, continuing to fellowship with the saints. We truly enjoyed the people the Lord had put in our lives. Shortly after our move, I became pregnant again. This time I wanted a girl. I somehow allowed myself to be convinced that having my child at home would be a wonderful experience. I knew of some women who had their babies delivered by a midwife and I thought this was what I should do. Insurance wasn't the problem because the Power Company had an excellent insurance plan. I just figured this would be good for me because I hated to be confined in labor. Both of my previous experiences were (in my opinion) too confining. I should probably have read Proverbs 4:17:

> *Wisdom is the principle thing, therefore get wisdom,*
> *and with all thy getting, get an understanding.*

I went into labor late one evening. I did enjoy having my baby at home more. It was better than my experiences in the hospital had been. Everything was so natural. Everything. One of my friends came (she was a nurse) to help me. So there was my friend, my husband, the midwife and an aide. With my last push, I waited for the great announcement of my daughter. My friend joyfully said, "It's a boy!" A boy? I already have two of those. Oh well, a real blessing was that it was my birthday.

Something was wrong. The midwife told me there was a blood clot but not to worry. She assured me that it would pass. She said the same thing had happened to another woman and the clot passed. Well three days later the clot obviously hadn't passed. I called my husband at work and told him I needed to go to the hospital. Well, (those of you with weak stomach might want to skip this part) I decided to remove the clot myself. (*Now* I decide to get brave). I became a bit alarmed because I could hear flesh tearing. My husband took me to the emergency room and the nurses agreed it was a blood clot but when the doctor came he firmly stated, "This is not a blood clot, this is her cervix!" He didn't attempt to do anything. He told me that he needed to call an OB/Gynecologist immediately! There happened to be a very respected doctor available because he had just delivered a baby. He examined me, looked into my eyes and said, "This is why we have babies in the hospital. If this had happened in a delivery room, it could have been repaired immediately." He attempted to repair the damage but to no avail. He looked at me again and said, "I have to take you immediately to surgery. I may have to perform a hysterectomy." By now, tears began to roll down my face. How could I have been so foolish?

I don't recall how long I was in surgery. Afterwards, the doctor told me he had done his best. He hadn't performed a hysterectomy, but he informed me that we would have to wait and see if further surgery would be required. Needless to say, he discouraged me from considering the prospect of any more children. I was hurt and very weak. The doctor sent me home.

The next few hours were very frightening. My mother-in-law came to get my older boys so my husband could attend to the baby and me. I began to cough uncontrollably. Each time I would cough, I would lose a lot of blood. I would call for my husband who was taking care of the baby in the other room because I was too weak to care for myself. He would change me, change the bed repeatedly, and take care of the baby. I called the Doctor around midnight because the process seemed endless. He said that I had to make it through the night and there was nothing else that could be done. I cried out to God because it seemed that I was dying. The Spirit of the Lord entered the room and he said, "Weeping will endure for the night, but joy will come in the morning." My husband continued to care for us. I could see the weariness in his eyes, but he never complained and, just as the Lord promised, morning came and the hemorrhaging ceased.

The Change

Although we continued to go to church, something was wrong. I didn't know exactly what. My husband's late night television-watching was becoming more frequent and I was very concerned, but I tried not to be a nag about it. I had so much to be thankful for, so why complain. I prayed and hoped this too would pass.

> **Note:** Something did happen but I didn't find out until several years later. My oldest son told me that he had a vision. In this vision, a demon came and told him that he would be around for a while. He told him not to tell his mother and if he did, he would cut his father's head off. The demon showed my son his father's head being cut off and his body being dragged away. He told me years later that he was afraid to tell me at first, and after a while he just forgot. At least four to five years had passed before my son shared this vision with me.

One day, the Lord instructed me to go outside and tell my husband something very specific. I realized then that maybe something was happening to him and to us. He loved working in the yard, so that's where I found him. He was busy tilling the ground. I said, "The Lord wants me to tell you something." He seemed interested so I didn't hesitate. "There are two things that you will never be able to change: The color of your skin and *His* call on your life." My husband just looked at me and never responded. I suppose I was hoping that with that word from God, his internal struggle would diminish. I hoped this would give him direction. I continued to be what I considered was a good wife, mother and servant of the Lord.

A few days later something strange happened. My cousin, who owned the house, had died and the executor of her estate (who was also a cousin) came to visit. This was not unusual since she was also a relative. We had a good visit and just as she was leaving she turned to me and said, "You are getting out of this house!" I was shocked.

"What happened? I said, why?" She really didn't give me a reason. I could see that something odd had happened and that the gift I wanted to operate in wasn't working. I asked her when we had to move and she said, "Start looking now." Her son was with her and he just looked at me, apologized as if he couldn't figure it out either, and they left.

I was devastated. We were only paying $100.00 a month for rent which was, of course, a wonderful price for a house. Where would we go? How could we find a decent place to stay with three children, on our income? I know, I know you're thinking, "Get a job!" I had gotten so used to being there with my children, spending time ministering to people, and being a wife. Besides that, my husband wanted me to stay at home.

I sought the Lord fervently. I did have fear within, but I couldn't show it. I prayed as we combed the rent section of the newspaper. I repented daily for filing bankruptcy. Every house we found, we couldn't afford. I felt desperate and my cousin was relentless. One morning, as I was driving to the bank, I saw a "for sale" sign in the yard of a beautiful two-story house. The Lord said, "Stop there."

I said, "No, we can't afford that house."

He said, "Stop now." I did. My boys and I got out of the car and a really nice man came to the door. He told me that he buys houses, remodels them, and then sells them. He said his health was failing, however, and he just wanted to get out of the note. He gave me a tour. The house was breathtaking. I had never even hoped for something like this. He informed me that a letter-carrier had looked at the house and had $10,000 to put down, but hadn't yet. The man said if I was interested he would hold it for me until I could talk to my husband. All he wanted was $100.00 for good faith to hold it until late that evening. At that time, I was selling Tupperware so I had the money I was going to deposit. I gave him the cash. My husband loved the house and we were to meet this gentleman at his bank on Monday morning. That was on a Friday, so I had all weekend to worry.

Now, this was 1983. When we met the gentleman at the bank Monday morning, all the bank officer asked for was my husband's social security number and his place of employment. It was an assumable loan so all we needed to do was to get proof of insurance and pay some fees. That's it! God moved. We moved.

Back to Work

Shortly after we moved, I became employed. It was hard to leave the boys but I will admit it felt good to go to work and interact with people on a daily basis. Little by little, I began attending church more frequently without my husband. He was still good to us, but I could feel a wall building between us so, unconsciously, I built my own wall.

I was working at a pharmacy and learning a lot about medication that was fascinating to me. A gentleman, who was a therapist in private practice in the building next door, would often chat with me as I waited for the pharmacist to come and open for the day. In one of our conversations, I must have told him I had a degree. A year later, when he assumed the position as Director of a Mental Health agency, he called me one day to tell me about an opening. I hated leaving the pharmacy, but I jumped at the chance to work there. To me, this was a part of the gift I so strongly desired. I envisioned myself setting the captives free. I knew that a lot of the individuals were tormented and I wanted to help them. We had a family friend who was schizophrenic, and I cared a lot for him.

I was still going to church with our sons. My husband went with us sometimes and sometimes he didn't. I knew that he would be all right and I was still determined to fulfill the call on my life. I didn't understand what was happening to him and perhaps he didn't either.

My youngest son's Godmother and I were very close. God used us to minister to others and I was in heaven. I had a job that I loved; my children were happy; and my marriage would be all right because I believed my husband would be back in the place where he used to be. We were drifting apart, but I hoped this would turn around soon.

I was learning so much on my job. I silently prayed for the clients I worked with. I had a caseload of about sixty individuals, classified as chronically mentally ill. I am not exaggerating when I say, I loved my job. God had anointed me to bring a little peace to those who were grievously tormented. I felt so alive. I had a strong desire to see God deliver many of the people I worked with. I listened to their stories. Even when they were hallucinating, I was always intrigued. My job to me was more of a ministry. How can you love going to work as much as I did?

At one point, I began to wonder if my husband's real struggle was due to the fact that I was working and he had always wanted to be the sole provider. I had to work and I enjoyed working, but things had changed. I was relatively happy in all areas except my relationship with my husband. There was no real intimacy, and the enemy began to use that against us.

Apparently he was hurting and I became defensive. We were going through the motions. Most people, on the outside, could not detect that we were drifting apart. He just didn't seem like the man I married. Where was the man God had given to me? He looked the same on the outside, but I knew him and something was wrong. I missed him, although I probably didn't show it. For the first time in our marriage, I began to feel really insecure. Perhaps there was something wrong with me. I didn't know how to deal with my insecurities, but I didn't want to appear weak. I couldn't allow myself to focus on what appeared to be rejection, so I kept busy. Somehow, I grabbed an invisible armor. I wanted to be strong; I had to be strong. I suppose, in my own way, I began to shut my husband out just as he was shutting me out. I didn't know how to reach him. I couldn't understand what was happening to him

Old Wounds—Old Habits

When I was in high school and college I always felt I was too thin. I always wanted a better body shape and never really felt good about myself. I had a lot of childhood wounds buried deep within, but had never felt insecure before with my husband. He had always made me feel as if I was special, so right for him. Whenever I spoke of my imperfections, he was always so reassuring. I hated how I felt but I could always bury my feelings when I was at work because I loved my job. I supposed that, to him, loving my job meant that I didn't need him anymore. I certainly loved my job, but I loved him more than any job. I had gone back to work to lift the financial burden from his shoulders. The pharmacist who interviewed me when I re-entered the workforce, told me the primary reason he had hired me was a statement I had made in my interview. When he asked me why I wanted to return to work, I told him that I wanted to help my husband. He said he had never heard anyone say such a thing. He also told me that I was overqualified, but he felt he had to hire me because of the strong desire I had to help my husband.

I tried to start conversations with my husband about his feelings but he would always brush me off like there were no problems. Although I was fulfilled as a professional working woman and a mother, as well as by my commitment to God and his service, I was very lonely. I began to confide in a friend from the church.

My friend had been saved longer than I had, so I trusted her advice. I began to share my frustration and loneliness. She gave me some advice that thoroughly confused me. She told me that she was sure that it was all right with God if I got a male friend on the side and that I needed to be fulfilled as a woman. She also told me not to let it interfere with my marriage, instructing me not to get emotionally involved. WHAT? She was a married woman and I respected her, as well as her mate. I just looked at her, confused. Suddenly there was a conflict going on inside me and I hadn't had this struggle in years. Part of me was very much tempted to follow through with her suggestion. "Where was this coming from?" I thought. I had left that person behind (so I thought) years ago. My childhood wounds had caused me to become sexually promiscuous and my college days were filled with experiences that I was ashamed of. I had not once considered looking at another man in a sexual way since I was filled with the Holy Ghost. My husband had been all that my heart had desired until this moment.

I pondered what she had said over and over. (My biggest mistake) I didn't realize that I needed to cast down my imagination:

[In as much as we] refute arguments and theories and reasonings and every proud and lofty thing that sets itself up against the [true] knowledge of God; and **we lead every thought and purpose away captive into the obedience of Christ (the Messiah, the Anointed One).** 2 Corinthians 10:5 Amplified

She came to me a day or two later and told me that she had discussed with her husband, the things we had talked about. He was in agreement that she had given me the right advice, as long as I didn't get too serious. There truly is power in agreement.

Once I had allowed the enemy to put the thought in my head, it was easy for him to send someone my way. That someone didn't come from afar. Three blocks away was a new family friend of ours who was in the process of a divorce. This friend came by often, always spending time with both my husband and myself, never just with me. One evening, the three of us were talking in our kitchen. He often came by to talk because he was lonely and hurting. The friend suggested that we all go for a ride. I suppose he was restless. What happened next floored me. My husband suggested that I go for a ride with the friend. I looked at my husband in shock. He used to preach about abstaining from the appearance of evil. Whatever happened to the scripture,

Leave no room or foothold for the devil (give no opportunity to him) Ephesians 4:27 Amplified

He continued to tell me to go for a ride with this man. My mind was in turmoil. Why would he want me to do this? I tried not to overreact. He had often told me that I did, so I gave in. Our friend and I rode around and talked for a while. Then he said,

"Doll, I can tell you're lonely." Did I have a big sign plastered on my forehead? How did he know? I suppose this is the time that I needed the gift of discerning of spirits to be operating, but all that was operating were my emotions. Naturally, I replied yes and he let me know that he was lonely also. First, he hugged me. Next he kissed me. I didn't want this to be happening but I didn't resist either. I was so grateful that it was not possible to go any farther. We both suspected that we'd better get back.

The next thing that happened was as strange as what I had just experienced. When we walked into the house, the look on my husband's face was shocking. He looked at me with a smile. It chilled me. It was as if he knew and he was pleased. After the friend left, he asked me what we talked about. He didn't seem to be interested in any conversation I had with the friend. The next question he asked almost knocked me off my feet. He asked, "Did you kiss him?" I lied and lied and lied. I couldn't understand what was happening to me. He knew I was lying and he seemed pleased that I had gotten myself in this situation.

The friend began to call me at work and I enjoyed the attention. He talked, and I listened. We met and talked, and I listened. By now, my husband was paying me little to no attention. One night the friend and I decided to meet. I knew that I was wrong but I began to justify the behavior. (I know, I'm the only one.) I finally came to myself and began to pray. Driving home from work, I cried out to God. I begged him to please help me because I knew that I shouldn't do this. I pleaded for God to please help me because I didn't think I could help myself. At that time, I was taking an aerobics class and I made up my mind that I wasn't going. I was so proud of myself but when it came time to leave my husband asked me why I wasn't going to class. I told him that I didn't want to. Well, he literally pushed me out the back door, locked it, and stood at the door so I couldn't get back in. This is going to sound crazy, but I said with tears in my eyes, "God, you must want me to sin."

I met the friend as previously planned. I got into his car and we just drove around for a while. It's strange to say this, but I actually felt as if I didn't have a choice. I kept silently talking to God, fully aware that I was going to sin. Out of nowhere, the friend said, "Doll, I was reading my Bible today, plus you and your husband are my friends. We can't do this." I couldn't believe it. I began to thank God.

Let me interject something, dear friends, it has taken me years to get an understanding about a lot of the things that have happened to me over the last fifteen years. The Lord revealed to me that I was set apart to be the wife for his chosen vessel. He had anointed a man to be my husband, and I was anointed to be his wife. My husband's strength covered my weaknesses and my strength covered his. When my husband walked with the Lord, he provided the covering that I needed. It was God's divine plan for our childhood wounds to be healed, so God had snatched me out of the world to save my life. He had provided a man to love and care for me, as Christ loved the church. Ephesians 5:25 says;

> *Husbands love your wives even as Christ also has loved the church and gave himself for it.*

Dear friends, it is always God's divine plan to heal and restore our souls from the damage inflicted upon, and within, us as little children. God knows the atrocities we witnessed and experienced that so many of us cannot articulate. He has a plan for your deliverance and a purpose for your life. He will work all things together for your good no matter how bleak the future seems.

God was the covering for my husband and my husband was my covering. When he started to backslide he began to lose his anointing to cover me. As my covering left, I became exposed to the elements. I had not prepared for this winter season of my life because in my relationship with this man of honor, there was always some type of summer breeze no matter what problems I faced. In my nakedness and vulnerability, I began to reach for what was familiar to me to provide a covering. I wanted shelter.

I suppose some of you are wondering why I needed so much strength. I guess you are puzzled about whether or not I had a father. What could leave a woman so vulnerable? I am not at liberty to share everything. However, in spite of my childhood scars, one incident remained etched in my soul. As a young girl (about age thirteen), I attended a 4th of July function at the church. I arrived a few minutes earlier than many of the youths. I went to the fellowship hall where I discovered there were only adults preparing the meal. I, of course, didn't want to be where they were, so I turned and proceeded back through the church to go outside. The church pastor followed me. That didn't bother me because he had always been a family friend and he was like a father to me. As I approached the door, he came closer and began to fondle me. I froze. As he began to tell me how I was starting to develop, my feet finally began to move and I bolted out the door. I was too afraid to tell anyone for a long time.

After a long while, I confided in my oldest sister who was about twenty-three years old at the time. I made her promise that she wouldn't tell. Why did I think no one would believe me? My sister betrayed me and told my mother. (She actually didn't betray me but that's how I felt as a young child). My mother called for the Pastor to come to our house. My parents were with the Pastor in the kitchen and I could hear my mother questioning and threatening him. The pastor denied the incident over and over again. I was so afraid. When my mother called me into the kitchen, they looked like giants to me. No one came and stood by my side so I stood there shaking, alone. My mother asked me if the Pastor had touched me and I replied, "Yes." He called me a liar, but I looked *at* ~~and~~ him and said, "Rev.——- you know I'm not lying." My mother sent me out of the room, *and* what I heard next burned deep into my soul. My father began to shout loudly, "She's a liar. She's a liar. I don't believe anything she says. She makes up so many fictitious things. She's a liar." From that day on, no one ever spoke to me about the incident. No one ever came to see if I was all right or to tell me that they believed me.

I continued to go to that church until I was twenty-one simply because it was the family church and as a minor I had no choice. I had to face the pastor at every church function. I had to keep his secret, to protect his honor. Why is that the responsibility of a child? Even as I write this book, I realize there are some who will probably feel as though I should not have shared this. First of all, God has told me to share my experiences to set the captives free. Second, as children of God we sometimes protect the adult (who should be the stronger one) and leave the injured child to protect the honor of one who has damaged their soul. What messages do we silently give our children when they are abused? Are we telling them the adult is weak, so they must be strong? This idea was etched into my mind as a small child and resurfaced in my adult-hood. Was I taught to take abuse and keep silent? (My next book will describe that journey.)

So many times I have listened to adults justifying their wrong behaviors with the statement, "I'm a grown-up." My response is always the same to them, "Being grown-up does not make you right!" Being grown-up does not give us a license to abuse, hurt or mistreat others. Being grown-up does not give us a right to fulfill the lusts of the flesh, justifying it because of age. Adults have a responsibility to walk uprightly and to obey our heavenly Father. I recognize we will make mistakes. We are made of flesh and **no good thing dwells in our flesh, (Romans 7:18).** As we become more rooted and grounded in the Word, we will have more tools to resist the urges to gratify the lusts of our flesh. Romans 13:11-14 states:

> *Besides this you know what (a critical) hour this is, how it is high time now for you to wake up out of your sleep (rouse to reality). For salvation is nearer to us now than when we first believed (adhered to, trusted in, and relied on Christ, the Messiah).*

> *The night is far gone and the day is almost here. Let us then drop (fling away) the works and deeds of darkness and put on the (full) armor of light.*

> *Let us live and conduct ourselves honorably and becomingly as in the (open light of) day, not in reveling (carousing) and drunkenness, not inimmorality and debauchery (sensuality and licentiousness), not in quarreling and jealousy*

> *But clothe yourself with the Lord Jesus Christ (the Messiah) and* **make no provision for (indulging) the flesh** *(put a stop to thinking about the evil cravings of your physical nature) to (gratify its) desires (lusts)* Amplified

I wonder if our willingness to keep silent is an indication that we are covering our own secrets. Perhaps we justify by misinterpreting the scripture, **Love covers a multitude of sins** (I Peter 4:8) I believe that once the sin has been brought to the light, love steps in and provides a covering and giving the person the opportunity to be healed and delivered. James 5:16 instructs us to:

> *Confess to one another therefore your faults (your slips, your false steps, your offenses, your sins) and pray (also) for one another, that you may be healed and restored (to a spiritual tone of mind and heart). The earnest (heartfelt, continued) prayer of a righteous man makes tremendous power available (dynamic? it's working).* Amplified

The Word specifically states that in order to be healed and restored from our faults, we must confess. Without the proper treatment of any infection, that infection will spread. If we ignore the infection it can become deadly enough to kill us. Make no mistake; an untreated problem is causing many people a lot of serious pain.

Now you understand one of the reasons it was not hard to leave when I was filled with the Holy Ghost. I suppose you can also see why, as a Man of God, my husband was the tallest man I knew. He believed in me. He protected me. He covered me.

God knew that the enemy had set me up. That's why he made a way of escape for me.

Can you believe that sometime later when my husband and I discussed these incidents, he told me that he had known what was happening and had wanted it to? He said, he had wanted me to fall

33

so that he could use me as an excuse to (as he put it) fool around. THAT'S WHY HE PUSHED ME OUT THE DOOR!

Survival

As my marriage began to deteriorate, I protected myself by focusing on my church commitment, my children and my job. Meanwhile, my husband and I talked about divorce with every disagreement we had. I didn't want a divorce, I just wanted him back, but I couldn't figure out where he was. I began to nit-pick and criticize and so did he. We always gave one another the impression that we could make it on our own. Inwardly, I was afraid to be alone and divorce, to me, meant to fail. I couldn't face all of the gainsayers who were waiting to say I told you so. Besides, I loved him even though it was more and more difficult to show it.

My husband and I were going through the motions. I prayed and hoped things would turn around for us, assuring myself that I would get my husband back. There were times I was encouraged as he talked to me about the Word. He could still quote scriptures and expound on many truths in the Word. I would ask him questions and, somehow, he and I would get the understanding of certain scriptures. I could see the light in his eyes when he talked about the Lord. Sometimes, late at night, he would turn to me in bed and say, "Let's sing some church songs." He had such a nice voice and we harmonized well. He would sing tenor and I would sing bass. I didn't really sing bass, but we used to laugh because I could sing low notes and he could reach the higher ones. While at Pastor Boyd's church, we got many requests to sing a song entitled, "With a Made Up Mind." That song had so much meaning for us and meant so much to us and we meant what we sang. At least, we did at that particular time. We would look into one another's eyes and sing:

With a made-up mind, with a made-up mind
I'm willing to go, all the way through
And if it cost my life, I'm willing to pay the price
I've got heaven in my view

And if it means that I, have to walk alone
Or that my friends they may be few
I'm not going to worry about what others may say or do
I've got heaven in my view

We knew that our minds were made up to serve the Lord with all of our hearts. So, what was happening to us? That light in his eyes was growing dimmer and dimmer.

I never intended to mask my pain with my job but I did. I never wanted to become a liberated woman, but I didn't seem to have a choice. I began to attend more and more church functions, went to concerts alone, and loved being in the presence of the Lord and fellowshipping with wonderful people. Since my husband didn't seem like my husband anymore, I had to be strong for my children and myself.

Chapter Two

The
Journey

As I began to delve into my career, I soon gained the respect of my co-workers. I listened intently to those who had more experience in the field. I wanted to learn all that I could both naturally and spiritually. After I had been there for over a year, I went to a seminar. That seminar turned my whole life upside down.

I accompanied my supervisor (who I was very fond of *of whom I was very fond*) and a co-worker to a seminar about helping mental health consumers. The speaker had so much energy and knowledge and I sat at my table thinking, "I can do what she is doing." I could see myself traveling the country as an advocate for the mentally ill. To me, life just couldn't be better.

During the morning break, I made my way through the crowd to talk to the speaker. This was something that I had never done, but I had to let her know my plans. I wanted to know how she got to this level because that's what I could see myself doing. (Not bad for a housewife with no previous career goals. Needless to say, my parents would be relieved to see me doing something with that college education). She was friendly and very encouraging. That was it. I planned to keep in touch. I had a clear vision and there was no stopping me now.

After lunch, there was a new person at our table. He was an older gentleman whose daughter was schizophrenic. At the afternoon break, just as I was about to go to the ladies room, he stopped me. He seemed friendly enough, but I was going to make this conversation quick because I wanted to get back to the session on time. Stopping to listen to him was the biggest mistake of my life.

He introduced himself to me, saying, "I'm a Christian." He then had my full undivided attention. It was as though I had opened the door to my soul when he said that. He had a very gentle voice and spoke with deep concern about his daughter. As I listened to him and it seemed like my legs couldn't or wouldn't move. As he continued to talk about his daughter, I started to lose my mind. I wanted to scream, but I couldn't move or talk. I literally couldn't move. Panic took over my soul. He walked away as calmly and quietly as he had when he first came up to me. I tried to shake myself, but it didn't help. It felt as if my mind was leaving me and I was powerless to do anything.

I can't remember if I even knew to call on Jesus. My world, as I knew it was spinning. I tried to regain my composure as I slowly walked back to my table. I honestly don't recall if he was at the table when I made it back. I sat down for about a minute and then ran out of the conference. I was in a panic and didn't know what to do. I finally went back in and motioned for my supervisor. She quickly came to me and asked what was wrong, but I couldn't explain what was happening. I'll never forget what she said to me. I was well known in my hometown by my nickname, so she said, "Doll, your problem is you're too religious. You need to lighten up and live a little." I was so desperate and afraid that I was open to anything to get rid of this feeling. I asked her what she meant. She told me that I was too perfect, that I didn't drink or curse and that I was too much of a good girl.

She held onto me and assured me that I would be all right. When I got home I tried to explain to my husband what had happened. I couldn't make him understand how I felt. I was losing my mind and I couldn't stop it.

The next day at the seminar was the same. Something really strange was that the gentleman was not there and he didn't return. "God, what is happening to me?" I prayed, cried, prayed, begged, cried and prayed some more. Nothing worked. Then, my husband began to drink. I felt powerless and desperate. I was losing my mind and my husband. I wasn't physically losing my husband but he just wasn't the same.

Every routine thing became a chore for me. God wasn't answering. The heavens were like brass and I couldn't find any relief. I felt like God had forsaken me. I didn't have any more dreams. I just wanted to have a sound mind. Nothing changed. No one I talked to could help. I began to rehearse what my supervisor had said. I need to live a little, that's got to be it, I thought. I'm doing all of the right things and it's just not working. Actually, I was getting worse. I cried all the time. Now, my husband was drinking even more and staying out. Initially, he wasn't staying out late, but for him not to be home in the evenings was unusual. More and more he would stay away from home, using the fact that I wasn't the same as his excuse. Perhaps he felt inadequate because he couldn't fight my unseen opponent.

I felt like a timebomb. I didn't want to lose my mind and my husband, but I couldn't find any relief. So, I started to drink with him. I hated the taste but I wanted to escape. I wouldn't drink hard stuff, I was too afraid, so I just consumed wine coolers and daiquiris. Oh, my husband seemed to enjoy making me a daiquiri at night because I needed it to sleep. I hated to go to work now. The more I was around my clients, the worse torment became.

Since, my husband drank I would hide a wine cooler in a special place in the refrigerator, so he couldn't find it and I would have it to drink as soon as I got home. One day, after arriving from work, I went right to the spot I had hidden it. I couldn't find it. I was out of control with panic. I needed it. What was I going to do? I felt so out of control that I was afraid of myself. I begged God to please help me; I didn't want to become an alcoholic. The alcohol didn't make the torment go away anyway, but now I was craving it. Again, I cried out to God to please help me. A few minutes later I looked back in the refrigerator only to see the wine cooler just where I had left it. That was the last time I ever drank. I was tormented, but I didn't want to ever be that out of control again.

Joy in the Morning?

I was very familiar with the scripture: "Weeping may endure for a night, but joy comes in the morning." (Psalms 30:5 KJV). I remembered that scripture from my youth, however the mornings were always terribly frightening for me. Each day as I awakened, my body would tremble with fear. The shakings were like severe seizures. Many mornings I would get as close as I could to my husband. I would ask him to hold me just so the shaking would stop. In the beginning, he would hold me and attempt to comfort me, but after a while he wouldn't allow it. I realize now that he felt helpless to fight this invisible giant. As time progressed, I would try to ease next to him while he was in a deep sleep so that he wouldn't detect my closeness. I suppose I felt like I was gaining some type of strength from him, sort of like charging a dead battery. It is very difficult to describe how difficult it was to be too petrified to place my feet on the floor and face another day. The convulsions became a constant occurrence throughout my journey.

At this point, I could only rely on the Word that had been placed within me. My Bible became foreign to me. It was as if a lock had been placed on it. Prior to all this happening to me, I could read and memorize scriptures. Now, I could only stare at the words. They couldn't penetrate. The words that had once been my comforts, my friends were now like strangers. Even as a little girl, I can remember reading the Bible at night. I would read pages and pages and it didn't matter to me that some of the things I read were difficult to comprehend. I suppose, as a child, I had hoped that I was destined for something great. My spirit would leap within just from reading the word.

Desperation and despair became my companions. This experience seemed like it was drawing me into a deep pit and I was powerless to stop it. It challenged my reasoning. It challenged my foundation. I remember confusion settling deep within my mind. I began to question the existence of Jesus. I recall turning to my husband one morning and pleading with him for truth about Jesus. At one point I asked, "Is Jesus really real?"

Not realizing at that time that he was in a battle for his own soul as well, he looked at me and shouted, "Don't ask me, I don't know!" Now, it seemed like all hope was gone. I had needed to hear him say "yes." I needed something to hold on to and I wanted to hold on to the Jesus that I had come to love. Now, nothing was real anymore. Nothing.

I must interject at this point that this is difficult to write and recall. My hands are trembling as I press every key. Oh, I don't question the authenticity of my Lord and Savior. I know the Power of God is real and Jesus is ALIVE because he lives within me. My struggle is in remembering the bowels of hell that engulfed me for such a long time. It pains me to recall all of the torment, but the Father has said it is now time to tell of the journey. This is not for me but for you, dear friend. This is to give you insight about the powers of darkness and the Power of Light. This is to help that family member whom you don't understand or that friend that drains the life out of you for answers that you can't find. Day after day, people are drawn to me. They find themselves sharing things that they say they cannot share with anyone else. They feel like they are crazy and believe they are losing their minds. I don't always have an answer for them, but most of the time they are relieved that I understand, and the weight of their trial becomes a little more bearable. Somehow, even in the midst of their trial, they at least have the hope that this trouble won't last always.

The Search for Answers

The ministers of the church I was attending were led to relocate, and now I began the process of finding a church to help me. What a winding road. Church was in me. I knew form and fashion from my Baptist background. I knew shouting and dancing and watching the gifts in operation. I had attended African-American churches, predominantly Caucasian churches, and racially-mixed churches. I had experienced the gamut. I fellowshipped wherever I could get the truth.

Every church always had the answer for me (so they said). One minister told me he had experienced the same problems I was having and he was now free. He laid hands on me and assured me that it was over. I was encouraged but somewhere deep, deep within I knew that it wasn't over. Something within began to tell me that even he wasn't free from whatever his struggle had been. I dismissed that voice because I couldn't bear to believe my torment wasn't going to end. By now, it had been over a year and I was still getting worse.

I went to a therapist who was very kind and understanding. He was certain that this would be over shortly, and quickly informed me that it was only my wounded child within. At one of our sessions he indicated that I was experiencing side effects from taking birth control pills. With that information, I scheduled an appointment to get a tubal ligation. Now, all I had to do was get my tubes tied, stop taking the birth control pills and stand up for myself a little and it would be over.

I did what the minister said and what the therapist advised. Nothing changed. Absolutely nothing. My mother sent someone from her church to talk to me. I knew in my heart that it wouldn't help. Actually, I was afraid to talk to him. I knew from my childhood experiences that the Word as I had come to know it was not taught there. I knew my torment would get worse. I was right. It got much worse. In the process I was learning some things, but I didn't realize it at that time. When certain people tried to help me, the power of the enemy on me got worse. I couldn't discern it at that particular time. I just knew that I would become more afraid and that the oppression would become stronger.

Let me explain to you what it felt like. On the inside, I walked in a state of panic. On the outside, it felt like I was carrying someone on my shoulders that weighed a ton. This thing on my shoulder had a strong grip on my head. There was something constantly speaking in my ear. There were times late in the evenings when it would get off my shoulders. Then, and only then, was there a little relief. It was always for a very short time. It seemed as if every morning it would fasten itself onto me when I put my feet on the floor. I know some of you are thinking, "Why didn't she just rebuke the devil? Why didn't she just plead the blood of Jesus." Dear friends, I did. And every single time I did, the power would bear down on me even harder. As I sought the Lord he would always only say, "My Grace is Sufficient for you"

And He said unto me, My grace is sufficient for thee: for my strength is made perfect in weakness. Most gladly therefore will I glory in my infirmities, that the power of Christ may rest upon me. 2 Corinthians 12: 4

I was not getting any better and a co worker recommended a psychiatrist. She told me that her mother had been depressed for years and this person had helped. I was so thankful for the recommendation, it gave me hope. I visited her office with such anticipation. She was an elderly woman with a kind smile and she reminded me of what a grandmother would be like. (I had never met my maternal grandmother, as she died when my mother was about five years old. My paternal grandmother was now deceased, but she had not been very motherly.) I felt safe. You must understand, I wanted and desperately needed to get some relief, and I needed her to have my answer. She confidently told me that I was chronically depressed and prescribed medication. I was almost happy that she gave my struggle a name. Chronic depression. I was relieved. Thank God, I'm only depressed.

I knew from working in mental health that medication can be very helpful. Now, I had another struggle; The church. The church had such a hard, hard teaching about medication, ESPECIALLY medication related to your mind and emotions. Oh, how the church hurt, confused, and condemned me on this issue. I have encountered countless individuals with the same struggle because of the church. I have never heard anyone encourage a diabetic to stop taking their insulin or someone suffering from high blood pressure to stop taking their medication. I have never encountered anyone encouraging kidney dialysis patients to skip their treatment. I have also never encountered anyone attempting to stop a cancer patient from getting their prescribed chemotherapy. However, I have experienced countless children of God judging people who are taking medication for their mind or emotions. This has caused people to walk in condemnation and guilt. They are made to feel weak and without faith. Yes, I know that there are those who may use their medication as a crutch. That is true and it happens. However, if they were healed from the root cause, perhaps they would get rid of the crutch. Please, please, seek God before you give advice to them. It is difficult to understand how they feel unless you have sat where they sit.

My psychiatrist told me that my problem was my mother.

Blessed (Happy, fortunate, prosperous, and enviable) is the man who walks and lives not in the counsel of the ungodly (following their advice, their plan, and purposes). Psalms 1 Amplified

I don't remember what we talked about in most of those sessions. My thoughts were always so jumbled. She told me in a round about way to stop letting my mother control me. Actually, she wasn't and never did control me. Let's compare notes. The first therapist said it was the child, the second, my mother. They both agreed on one thing. They strongly recommended that I take charge of my life. All of this information got so mixed up in my head. I needed an answer so, again, I made theirs the answer, a major mistake.

A Motherless Child

I took the medicine as prescribed, and I got a little relief from the panic but none for the weight on the outside. I was taking two different kinds of medication and was always being reassured that it would take time before they took effect. I did exactly as I was told but, to my dismay, nothing was changing.

I was invited to another church. I went up to the front for prayer, and the minister told me that he was once depressed and now was free. He challenged the spirit of depression and boldly told it to come against him and get off me. I was frightened beyond belief. I wanted this to stop for me but I was afraid for him. I couldn't understand why he was doing that. Fear turned to condemnation because he made it seem so easy. He seemed powerful and yet foolish. Several members of the church quickly came to me and told me that they needed to come and anoint my house. They came that afternoon and anointed everything, even the closets. Now, I knew it was over.

I soon discovered, however, that the worst was yet to come. Since that minister was so bold to challenge the depression I continued to go to that church. Strangely, soon thereafter, his wife died. He quickly remarried and relocated. Another minister took over. One Sunday night as church was ending, we were all in a prayer circle. I wasn't getting any better, so with each prayer anyone prayed I begged for relief. My eyes were closed and I suddenly felt my hands being jerked away from the people holding them. I opened my eyes and it was my husband. His shirt was open and he looked enraged. I cried out in my heart, "God, why would you let him embarrass me like this?"

He said, "Go to the hospital, to your mother." He went to get the boys out of children's church. As I got in my car, a peace came over me. I hadn't had any real peace for over a year. I did recall that earlier that day I had spoken a little harshly to my mother, but the peace was so comforting.

Immediately, I went to the emergency room and told them who I was. Since I was named after my mother, I didn't have to explain who I was coming to see. A doctor and nurse greeted me and took me to a small room. My peace began to slip away. What did they want? The doctor said, "I'm sorry, but your mother is dead." I screamed! They tried to calm me down, asking if I wanted to see her. They took me into another room where she lay under a sheet, but I wouldn't let them pull the sheet off her face. I couldn't take any more. I touched her body and felt the cold hardness of death. Now, my torment increased more than you could ever imagine.

Eli, Eli, lama sabachthani —-*MY GOD, MY GOD*
WHY HAVE YOU FORSAKEN ME?

My mother was gone. "How could this be happening?" I wondered. A young lady, walking down the street, had witnessed what we call a freak accident. My mother had just left church that night and had pulled up in her driveway. She always parked on the incline because my father wasn't home yet to put his car in the garage. As she was getting out of the car, she was apparently reaching for a sandwich she had purchased on her way home from church, when it began to roll. She had mistakenly put the car in reverse instead of park, and she was dragged by the car into the street. She was hanging on to the door or steering wheel, but she finally let go. While she was lying in the street, her car hit the curb lurched forward, and landed on her chest. My house wasn't far from hers and my sister-in-law, who lived next door to my parents, called my husband. When he got there, the car was still on her chest. He tried desperately to lift it off. She was already dead, but he wouldn't accept it and continued to try until he was restrained.

In spite of my pain, grief and torment, the family expected me to write her obituary. I was her baby, the minister, the peacemaker. My older brother and sister lived in other states so they didn't know how sick (as they termed it) I was. At this time, the Lord lifted the torment just enough for me to hear him clearly. He gave me the songs for the funeral, the scriptures to read, and even who was to eulogize her. I soon found out that the night before she died, the Lord had led someone to talk to her about the unforgiveness in her heart. She had been treated cruelly by individuals I will not mention. She forgave them and the next day, at church, she began to speak about the Power of God and the beauty of all of his creation. Even though I was in so much pain, this made me thankful.

When it was time for the family to go and view the body, my husband was too overcome with grief to even get out of bed. My brother and I had to dress him and take him to the mortuary. I don't recall him ever making it to the casket. He just sat in a pew and wept. When I saw my mother's face, IMMEDIATELY, the Lord spoke to me in a song. I could hear ringing in my soul, "It's all right, it's all right. Jesus said he'd fix it, now it's all right." I couldn't rejoice, but I gained a little comfort.

The Lord gave me the scripture: "To be absent in the body is to be present with the Lord" (2 Corinthians 5:18). He also led me to a song entitled, "I like it here, it's great to have the father of the universe so near." I had that song played at her funeral. When we entered the church, I looked on the chalkboard next to the choir loft, because when I attended that church the choir director would always write the songs for that Sunday on the chalkboard. I was surprised and blessed to see one of the songs that the Lord had told me to have sung at the funeral. It was the old Negro spiritual, "Hush." I could hear the words to that song ringing in my ear in the days prior to the funeral. It goes:

Hush, hush, somebody's calling my name,
  (repeated three times)
Oh my Lord, oh my Lord, what shall I do?

It sounds like Jesus; somebody's calling my name
Oh my Lord, oh my Lord, what shall I do?

When the funeral was over, I could hear the whispers from my family: "Something is really wrong with Doll." They had taken pictures of my mother in her casket (don't ask me why) and they made sure that I didn't know about it. They felt it would take me over the edge.

Things were so bad for me now that I wanted to just go ahead and lose my mind. The torment was beyond words. My husband was staying out and drinking excessively, and I was alone, completely alone. It seemed like the only thing I lived for now was my children. If I hadn't had them at that time I don't know if I could have pushed myself to get up in the morning.

I stopped seeing the psychiatrist. I guess I blamed her for my not talking to my mother. I found another therapist that I really liked except he was convinced that my problem was my husband. So, my child, my mother, my husband. I never told any of them about the man at the seminar. What would I say? How could I explain that?

With this new therapist came countless different medications. I took Deseyrel, Tofranil, Ascendin, Elavil and Xanax (no, not all at the same time). Only the anti-anxiety pills gave a little internal relief. At one point, I was taking so much medicine that, technically, I should not have been driving. Only the grace of God kept me from killing myself. I did want to die, but I didn't want to leave my children.

My mind was becoming more and more confused, but I got a little relief when I talked to this therapist. I didn't feel as tormented when I talked to him. He was a Christian and he had a gentle spirit. As soon as I left his office each time, the small relief was gone. He even gave me his home phone number and whenever I called him, he was patient and kind. He didn't always try to have the answers. Sometimes, he would just listen to me, and I needed that. I could even talk to him about demons. Sometimes I could see them flying around me. He never once said that I was crazy.

I tried everything he instructed me to do and everything the magazines said to do, as I searched diligently for the answer. I was told that if I exercised, it would help to alleviate the depression. I was instructed to take vigorous walks and I must have covered several miles per day. Every evening after I prepared dinner, my youngest son and I would walk. He was about three years old and he would practically run to keep up with me. I thought if I put my heart into it, surely I would get relief. My son never asked me to slow down. He would just run to keep up with me.

The walks brought more torment to me. On many occasions, as we walked, I would see the car that killed my mother. My father had sold it to someone in the area and my son would recognize it as "MeMaw's" car. Each time I saw the car I wanted to scream. I had to relive that night over and over again. I felt as though I was being pushed over the edge and Satan was laughing. There were times when I would change my direction but the enemy always knew my route.

Nonetheless, I was not getting better. One night, I grabbed one of my many prescription bottles and went to a room in my house. I was crying. I wanted out of this present life. I didn't want to live anymore. At least, not like this. Just as I was about to take the pills, someone shouted, "telephone." I can't even remember who it was but, today, I thank God for that call.

By now, even my therapist was worried about me. I decided to go to the hospital. I had watched my clients go there and at least become stabilized. I needed some answers and there were none to be found. My therapist believed I would probably kill myself, so he made arrangements for me to go to a private hospital that very evening.

The hospital was beautiful, not at all like I had imagined. I guess it was the Betty Ford hospital of that time. I felt I would get better and be my old self again. I kept hearing people say, "I want the old Doll back." I hated those words. It always felt as if they thought I was like this on purpose. By now, my husband was telling me how weak I was.

The Hospital

I was surprised that there were so many professional people at the hospital. Nurses, television technicians, businessmen, you name it, we were all there. The staff had a schedule of events to fill your day. We also had a psychiatrist, who added yet one more medication to what I was already taking. Once again, I was pulling on them for answers. I recall asking the psychiatrist if I had had a nervous breakdown. He said no, but that I was on the verge of one. Saints, isn't it amazing how we can get so close to the edge and even though we want to go overboard, the Lord will only let Satan go so far? I thank Him for that.

Well, I participated in every activity and session required, but to no avail. Something stranger began to happen: I started dying. Seriously, I began to die. I could feel life slowly leaving me. Even though I was still functioning, I knew that I was dying. There was no point in my going to a medical doctor. I did that in the beginning. I had every test imaginable and I was proclaimed healthy. Even when I had physical symptoms, all tests came back negative.

I could feel something drawing life out of me like a vacuum, but there was no way to prove it.

My husband brought our sons to see me. I had looked forward to seeing them but something happened that I will never forget. Their ages were only three, five and seven, but when I saw them approaching, I realized I had no feeling for them whatsoever. I stared and stared. I went through the motions, but they were like little strangers to me. I tried to feel but I couldn't. I continued, with all of what little strength I had to pretend because I didn't want to hurt them, but I was screaming within to God, "What is wrong with me? Help, me!" When they left, I was glad because it was so hard to go through the motions. My therapist told me I was suffering from burnout because I was trying to be a supermom.

My sister, Loretta, flew in from California to see me. My sister-in-law, Anna, left her job in Texas and went right to the airport without a change of clothing. Anna said she just had to come to me. I realized that she was the one who called my sister in California. They were convinced that I was sick because of our mother's death. I quit trying to offer explanations or find answers. I was tired of the fight. I knew they didn't have any answers for me. I overheard Loretta talking to my brother on the phone. She said, "Doll is so sick and I have never seen anything like this in my life. It's going to take a long time before she is all right."

I had a dream that night (I believe it was the night Loretta left). In the dream, I had given my children a party. I must have still been very sick and tormented because I couldn't participate in the activities. I just lay in the bed until the party was over. After the party, I got up to straighten the house. As I was cleaning, I saw a woman kneeling in prayer. Her head was bowed and she wore all white. Just when I got close enough to touch her, she looked up. It was my mother. I screamed, "Where have you been?"

"I've been praying for you," she replied, "you're going to be all right." Needless to say, I held on to those words for the next five years. That's correct. This most difficult part of my journey lasted seven years! The entire process for this ministry was fourteen years.

A Surprise Visit

Part of the daily schedule at the hospital was some type of physical exercise. One late morning, as a group of us were playing softball, I noticed a very familiar car entering the hospital grounds. I thought, surely that's not who I think it is. The car was very similar to my father's, but I knew it couldn't be his car. I had asked my husband not to involve my family as I was already ashamed of my struggle. Some of them would think I was a failure and I just couldn't deal with that.

It was my father. Why did I have to face him? Fear gripped me. As his car got closer I slowly walked over to it. He hadn't parked yet, but he asked me to get in. He looked at me and began to yell, "I refuse, I refuse, I refuse for this to be happening to you!" He told me that I was his daughter and I was a strong person. He said that he hadn't seen me for days and my husband had been evasive. My father had then pressured him into revealing where I was. I didn't say much. What could I say? It was apparent that he thought I had either had a nervous breakdown or was soon to have one.

It was time for lunch and he offered to join me. I really didn't want him to because eating was difficult for me and I hated it when people tried to force me to eat. Different people would remind me that I had to eat to live. I knew that, but I couldn't explain that I could barely swallow.

As we entered the cafeteria, he seemed pleased that the hospital was so nice. He even smiled with approval and commented on how pleasant it was. I knew that, somehow, the stigma of the state hospital was etched in his mind and I sensed this place was less embarrassing for him. I didn't talk much. I really didn't have much to say. I couldn't explain to him what was happening to me. He, too, believed that my "breakdown" was due to my crumbling marriage.

Get Out

With each passing day, I was dying. I called a couple of people to pray for me. I told them I was dying and to please pray. My cousin, Laura, called me. This cousin has always been, and still is, very special to me. Laura was the one who led me to Pastor Boyd's church. She had heard him preach at a tent revival and knew I would be blessed by his teaching. She also received the Baptism of the Holy Ghost on the same day that I did. We had shared a lot of joy and pain together through the years. When I heard her voice on the other end, I was glad it was her. We no longer lived in the same city, so I didn't get to see her often. Actually, at that time, she was a student at Oral Roberts University. Laura told me that she had been praying for me and the Lord told her that what was happening to me was all spiritual. She said, "Doll, God said you are going through a spiritual battle." She told me that she didn't understand the battle because the Lord didn't give her any details. I remember her words almost like yesterday. She said, "Baby, I'm praying for you." I held onto the assurance that she would pray until it was over.

I could not comprehend exactly what she meant about a spiritual battle. All I knew was that I was losing my mind, and the seasonal events seemed to cause the battle to become more intense. Halloween was approaching, and for some reason the battle seemed to be more intensified. I could feel the life slowly leaving my body as though a vacuum cleaner hose had been attached to my vital organs. I went home to visit my family for twenty-four hours. I felt like a zombie as I went through the motions. My husband mostly ignored me and wouldn't look directly into my eyes. I called a friend of ours to pray for me. Derrick served as best man at our wedding and he loved us. We had such a bond that he truly was our brother. He also had left his traditional church, years before, to fellowship with us at Pastor Boyd's church. I tried to explain my torment and I could feel his concern and panic. He pleaded with me to allow him to come and visit me in the hospital. I begged him not to because I was so embarrassed by what appeared to the saints as my lack of faith. I could hear the panic in his voice as he agonized for an answer that would help me. I heard months later that he went to church the next day and fell upon the altar fervently praying and crying for my deliverance.

When I returned to the hospital, my torment worsened. Somehow the Halloween season was taking its toll on me. The hospital was decorated with black cats and other types of Halloween decorations. As a part of our recreational time, we were required to carve a jack-o-lantern. I attempted to protest, but was continuously encouraged to participate. After all, everyone was participating except me, and I was constantly told that I needed to learn to have fun.

Fear fastened itself upon me and I was certain I would not make it out of the hospital alive. That very week, I received a call from Loretta's friend, Bill. Bill was very fond of me and I of him. To this day, he does not recall the conversation, but I know he saved my life. By now, I had been in the hospital for more than three weeks. I was progressively getting worse. My therapist from home had even come to visit me. God, I loved him. Anyway, Bill asked me how I was doing and I told him that I was dying. He very firmly said, "Get out of there, Doll. Pack your clothes and leave, now." My head was confused, but his voice resounded like a bull-horn in my spirit. It was the voice of the Father and I heard it loud and clear.

I couldn't just walk away, but the Lord gave me the strength to articulate well enough to convince the hospital I was well enough to go. By now, my hospital bill was about $30,000. If I just walked out, the insurance would find a reason not to pay. The Spirit of the Lord, deep within me, helped save my life. Two days later, I was discharged. I remember the anointing of the Holy Ghost speaking through me that last morning in the group therapy session. I don't remember what I said but I do remember tears in the eyes of all in the room, even the therapist, and she had always seemed detached and aloof. Praise God

Home Again

I returned home, but my feelings were still gone toward my children. I pretended day after day after day. That was the only real fight I had. I had to feel my love for them again. There was a shield over my emotions for them. I just couldn't penetrate the barrier.

My husband's friends began to come over quite frequently (when he was home) and remain until the early hours of the morning. They would talk loudly, drink, curse and listen to music. Other things began to surface as well. There was a particular young lady who considered herself my little sister. I had been her sister's classmate and she just loved being around me. I enjoyed her as well. I discovered that while I was in the hospital she and my husband became friends. She even came to cook for him and the boys while I was gone. Whenever I questioned him, he reminded me that there was something wrong with me. On one of the many nights he was out I went to find him. I located him at her apartment. I was still overreacting, he said, they were just friends.

I would beg him to stay home with me as I couldn't function and needed help. He would frequently say to me, "Stay home for what? I'm not going to sit around the house and hear you talk about the same stuff."

I returned to work in a different capacity. It was orchestrated by my therapist and I was grateful for that. It became more and more difficult to work. Not only was there something tormenting my mind and emotions, there was now something affecting my fine motor skills.

Each day I was required to write case notes. As I would attempt to write, something would jerk my pen across the page. I labored, in tears at time, just to write the client's name on the sheet. I no longer had an office, so I couldn't hide this affliction. My desk was adjoined with a co-worker's, who could see my struggle although she pretended not to. She, too, had a gentle spirit. I cried and cried as I clutched my pen with all of my strength to write a sentence. She brought me a plaque that reads, "All good things take time." Fourteen years later, that plaque remains an inspiration to me. It is in my office today. Wherever you are Judith, God Bless You. She was only there briefly, and she gave me that plaque and a book. The book described another woman's journey and it gave me a little hope.

My marriage was deteriorating right before my eyes and I was once again powerless to fight what came next.

Chicago

A dear cousin of mine was visiting her mother at the same time of my release from the hospital. Lorraine is an Evangelist and I greatly respect her ministry and anointing. She prayed constantly for me and trusted God to deliver me. She and my mother had been very close and I knew she felt committed to helping her cousin's youngest daughter get free.

Lorraine asked me to go back to Chicago with her for a few days. She strongly believed that if she could get me out of my environment, and to her church, I would change. She believed if her pastor prayed for me, then God would deliver me. I held on to her and trusted that this torment would be over shortly.

The ride to Chicago was long. We were traveling by automobile and many times during the trip she encouraged me to hold on. It felt as if I was slipping from reality. The struggle was so intense that I had a hard time concentrating. I believed that if I could keep my mind intact for just a few more hours, I would achieve the freedom I had begged God for.

Lorraine's church was in the midst of a revival and the saints were very friendly. She continued to encourage me to hold on, assuring me that her pastor would pray for me.

The first night of the revival, I don't recall an altar prayer, nor did the pastor minister to individuals in the congregation. I was discouraged. After church, I remember meeting the pastor but I didn't get prayer. This process continued throughout the week.

There happened to be another Evangelist in the area running a revival. We went to his service and this time I got prayer, but there was still no change. In fact, once again the oppression seemed worse. Desperation engulfed me. I couldn't continue to live like this. This was not the abundant life; it wasn't living at all!

Lorraine's youngest daughter, Jane, came to visit, but I had very little strength to converse with her. She has always been a dear, precious cousin who loves the Lord, but I just stayed in the bedroom trying to hold on to what little sanity I had left. I could hear the whispers of concern about me from the living room. Those conversations always pained me. I know that people were worried about me, but I was tormented, not deaf. I now know how seriously-ill individuals feel when they are surrounded by loved ones whispering about the severity of their conditions. I realize their conversations of concern are not meant to hurt, or to deepen the fears of despair. However, they reinforce the assignment of the enemy to destroy. Individuals who are in the trial of their lives need faith-filled words of encouragement that bring power and hope. They don't need the negative power of words agreeing with the conditions brought on by the enemy.

On the last night of my stay, we attended Lorraine's church again. The pastor called me to the altar for prayer. It seemed as if my feet were like lead as I pressed my way to the altar. The pastor began to pray for me and spoke words that pierced my soul: "Even if you see your husband (and she called him by name, which shook me) with another woman, hold on. God is going to work it out, so hold your head up." What? I certainly knew she had missed God. What about my torment? This is not what I needed to hear. What about this oppression? What is going to happen to me? I know God won't allow my husband to have an affair while I'm in this condition. I'm not strong enough to endure that!

The ride home seemed longer than the trip there. On the way to Chicago, I had a glimmer of hope about getting free, and now I was returning to the land of my affliction, with no improvement and no hope of deliverance.

I Want Out

Two months after I got out of the hospital, my husband said he wanted out. I couldn't believe this was happening to me. The beginning of this torment was June 1986, my mother died in March of 1987 and it was now January of 1988. He wanted out. He wanted me to find a place for the boys and me to live. He planned to walk away from the house and I didn't make enough money to maintain a house that large. His income was a lot higher than mine, but he was getting his own apartment. I know most of you are thinking that God gave me the house and I didn't need to go anywhere. He is obligated to take care of the children, etc. etc. I did meet with an attorney to file for a divorce, but as I was sitting there the Lord said, "Leave." I knew that the demons often said things to me but this was coming from my belly. Again, I heard, "Leave, no divorce." Then, I heard, "Get up now." I abruptly left, confused and afraid.

I was watching everything that I had, literally being snatched away from me and I could do nothing about it. I had to find another place to live. I was a failure. I didn't mean to get sick! In my wildest dreams I never thought my life could end up in so much turmoil. This was not supposed to happen to me. When I married my husband, one of his sisters threatened me. She called me and, very matter of factly said, "If you hurt my brother, I will hurt you." She felt that, with the age difference, I would more than likely discard her brother when I became bored with him. Now who is threatening him? No one. Whatever happened to our vows; for better or for worse; in sickness and in health; until death do us part? How could he leave me at the worst time of my life?

My world had fallen apart. I couldn't even hold on to one blessing from the Lord. I continued struggling to regain the feeling for my children. My appetite had left me months before and I thank God for my experience at the pharmacy. Because of it, I knew to drink Ensure, so I bought it by the case. Whenever I tried to eat it seemed as if my throat locked up and I couldn't swallow the food.

I continued to see my therapist when I got out of the hospital. He was now seeing me every day and he seemed to want me to get better as much as I did. One afternoon, I walked into his office and he had tears in his eyes. I quickly asked him what was wrong. He looked directly into my eyes and said, "Doll, I can't help you." I knew that I wasn't hearing him correctly! Not Gary! He can't desert me.

He can't leave me to myself. I knew he was a Christian, but we didn't talk about God all of the time so his next words dug deep into my soul. He said, "I was praying and the Lord said that I can't help you. He told me that very few people will go through a battle such as yours, to the extent that you have and will experience." Gary then told me that he knew he probably would never experience such a journey and was not equipped to help me. We both cried and I left. I have often wondered where and how he is. I hope our paths cross again on this side. If not, then I hope to see him in Glory.

Who Will I Talk To?

I looked forward to spending time with my therapist. At least he would listen and sometimes that helped my focus. Now, there was no one to whom I could pour out my heart without being reminded of how sick I had become.

One day, while praying God told me to call Sister Jacque. She was the sister that I had gotten close to at Pastor Boyd's church. It had been a very long time since I had seen her. As I began to tell her what was happening to me she understood everything. She had gone through the same kind of torment in the years we had been apart. She said she didn't have any answers. The Lord had not told her yet why she had such a journey. Nothing I told her surprised her. Even the crazy things that I did for relief she understood. She had experienced some of the exact same things. I told her about the time that something (I knew later it was Satan) had told me that if I had sex anytime my husband wanted to, I would be free. I know that some of you are thinking, "What is wrong with that." Well, by then, he had fully backslidden and the marriage bed had become defiled.

I told Jacque that my husband wanted out. I know it hurt her to see how vulnerable I had become. My mind was so mixed up that I honestly could not remember who Doll really was. I told her that I couldn't make it. She always encouraged me. She must have told me a thousand times, "Yes, you can make it; yes, you can do it." She helped me not to humiliate myself as my husband of nine years was walking out on us. I wanted to beg him not to leave me, but all I could do was go through the motions. I was talked out where he was concerned. Honestly, at times, the torment was even greater when he was around.

I recall a few days after I had gotten out of the hospital, I was sitting in the living room watching a movie with the boys. My husband hadn't come home from the night before and never bothered to call. I heard the back door open and a presence so strong and evil came over where I was sitting. I left my children, grabbed my blanket and ran upstairs. I grabbed the phone as I was hovering in the corner and called Lorraine. I told her what was happening and she began to pray. She said, "Doll, I believe Satan himself entered your house." Whether it was Satan, or a top ruling power, it was real. Years later, I mentioned the incident to my husband to see if he remembered. He told me, yes. He said he knew that he had something strong upon him and what it would do to me, but he didn't care.

Every single household chore now seemed impossible. If I could get one room vacuumed, that was a miracle. Just the thought of trying to cook any kind of meal, even to boil wieners, seemed like an impossibility. Daily, I would call Jacque crying. I would say I couldn't cook dinner, only to hear her say, yes, you can. Each small victory made me thankful.

Another Blow

The Lord led me to a nice development where I was able to rent a four-bedroom duplex. It was fairly new, spacious and subsidized, praise God. A couple of days after I found the duplex, my supervisor came to me and said, "Doll, the Director wants to see you." She had been kind and helpful to me and had worked with my therapist to find me what was supposed to be a less stressful position. It didn't make much difference, though, because each time I was around anyone who had really strong torment or demons, I felt it. Anyway, she said, "Doll, they are going to lay you off." She began to curse and kicked the door. She told me they had laid her off too. She told me to go in there, hold my head up, and not to let them see me cry. I was thinking "Why, God? What is the purpose of my existence on earth? There can't be a purpose left." I felt like God was standing by allowing the devil to kill me bit by bit. I was Satan's punching bag.

I tried to do as my supervisor had said (this was not the same one who had taken me to the seminar): hold my head up, right. To my amazement, God must have had an angel holding my head in place. The Director apologized and said this was a business decision. There were several individuals laid off, and my name was the last one on the list.

Let's recap: I'm tormented, my mother dies, I still have no feelings for my children, my husband wants out, I lose the house God gave me, and the job God gave me, I can't eat, and I can't sleep without sleeping pills. My children now have to enroll in a new school and make new friends; Everybody says I'm crazy and have had a nervous breakdown, and God won't let me kill myself.

My family was silently glad that my marriage was dissolving because they knew what was happening. They were also afraid that (as they put it) I would have another breakdown.

I watched my husband busy himself packing. He seemed so happy. I didn't talk. I just stared and hoped that he would change his mind and say he was making a big mistake. Some other things happened during the course of that evening that are just too painful to write. I doubt if I can ever talk about it openly. Anyway, I knew that I would lose my mind that night. Honestly, I wanted to. I had nothing left to live for, no purpose.

What Next?

My husband quickly moved us out and left to begin his life. I was unemployed and, in my opinion, in no shape to interview. I prayed and prayed. I constantly asked God why, and his reply was always the same, "Farther along, you'll understand why, and my Grace is sufficient for you." I didn't understand exactly what grace was, other than remembering the song the choir used to sing. The last line of their song about Grace says, "His Grace will give you the victory." I had practically given up on faith and hope. I suppose all I had was the Grace of God.

My former supervisor had been offered a job at another agency. She had a master's degree and felt the salary was not equivalent to her credentials, so she recommended me. I received a call from this agency and was asked to interview for a position. I struggled to stay lucid and it was a struggle. My mind seemed to be slipping away from me and I had begun to grocery shop late at night. I couldn't take the way people who knew me would stare at me. Sometimes, when I went to the store during primetime, the demons would tell me to run out of the store. I would hold on to the grocery cart for dear life, only to struggle when it came time to pay and I had to write a check. I would hold my pen so tightly and just pray. My penmanship was horrible. Eventually, I began to write as much information as possible on the check before I got to the grocery store.

Somehow, I dressed myself in a presentable way. With every step I took, the demons reminded me how much of a failure I was. They always told me that I would never make it, so I might as well give up. It's funny though because I could now feel that someone was praying for me. The torment was the same but I knew prayers were reaching the throne.

I entered the room for the interview only to discover that the interview would be conducted by four people. I didn't think I could take one. "Why four, God?"

The same reply, "My Grace is Sufficient for you." To my amazement, the Holy Ghost took over (I know the Holy Spirit and the Holy Ghost are one and the same, but to me, what I've been through, I feel an extra surge when I say the Holy Ghost). They seemed very impressed and I was just as impressed, as they were. It was as if the Lord would not let the demons go into the room with me.

They called me for a second interview and I had the same experience. The torment greeted me, however, whenever I left the room. Next, I had to take my youngest son to be tested for kindergarten. He was extremely restless and the counselor put some type of label on him. She gave a very negative prognosis on his ability to function in a regular class. Devastated again, I called Jacque. She listened and said, "Sister Doll, I believe God." Somehow with those words I began to feel a little hope for my son. Not for me, but for him. After six or seven months, my feelings slowly started to come back for my children and I loved this boy enough to start to fight for him. The interesting thing is that whenever I got the courage to begin to try to fight for myself, the torment got worse. I began to stand for my son. It was a wobbly stand, but it was the best that I could do. I found a scripture and quoted it daily. Whenever I heard the tester's words recited in my head, I said, "But Isaiah said, who has believed our report."

> *Who has believed our report, and to whom is the arm of the Lord revealed.* Isaiah 53:1

Jacque and her husband began to pastor the same church we had attended with Pastor Boyd. My boys and I began to attend. It was truly like going home. They had pretty much the same services as when we went before and one Sunday night, different people went up for prayer. My youngest son ran to the prayer line before I could stop him. He looked so out of place with all those adults. The torment was still heavy on me, so all I could do was sit there. When Sister Jacque laid hands on him she looked at me and said, "Sugar, Sister Doll take sugar out of his diet." This was years before all the reports came out about sugar and hyperactivity. As I type this book, I am currently not ingesting any foods with artificial sugars added. The Lord told me to fast sugar (candy, soda, etc.). He told me that artificial sugars feed fear in me. I have noticed, in my own life, that the more junk (candy) I eat the more I battle with fear. Quite frankly, I was afraid to begin this book. Well, I'm finally writing it.

I talked with Jeremy's teacher a couple of months after school began. She was not aware of the counselor's recommendation and she told me that Jeremy is a bright student. She said she had chosen him as student of the month. Today, as I write, Jeremy is the sophomore class president, an honor roll student, and he plays several musical instruments. Where would he be today if I had believed and received the negative report?

Crumbs

I truly didn't want to share the following experience. This unpleasant memory was something that I had tucked into the far corners of my past. The Father, however, brought it to the forefront and told me to share it. Even as I recall the incident, it pains me to realize how low my self esteem was.

Very soon after my husband and I separated, more fears and anxiety settled in. I felt as though I could not make it without him. I was afraid of parenting the kids alone; of facing the world and life's problems as a single parent; and of dealing with my torment without him with me. Although he was not helping me with the oppression, I still felt some sort of security just knowing that he was my husband. Many nights, before the separation, I would sit up and look out the window waiting for him to return. I would beg God to please send my husband home to me.

Early one morning, I looked out the back door and saw my husband's car in the driveway. He appeared to be asleep, so I went to the driver's side of the car only to see that the entire driver side was totally wrecked. I woke him up to see if he was injured. I thought maybe he was dead, so in a panic I began to shake him. When he awakened, he wanted to know what was wrong with me. I asked him what had happened and he had no idea how he had wrecked the car. He had been drinking heavily and only the angels of God had brought him home.

Now, to the crumbs. I didn't hear from my husband much for the first few days and weeks of our separation. I would call him just to hear his voice, but he was always so abrupt with me. He was beginning a new life that didn't include me. I could not take his rejection. He had dropped me, cold turkey, and the pain was unbearable. I drove to his apartment one afternoon. When I knocked on the door, it was obvious that he was not happy to see me, but that didn't deter me. He reluctantly let me in as he proceeded to get dressed to go out. By now it had become his custom to instruct me to follow him as I talked. I know now that I was feeding some type of spirit of self importance and control, but at that time I just needed him to talk to me. As I whined and pleaded with him to listen to me, he firmly let me know that I was not talking about anything of importance. My desperation was indescribable. At one point, I just sat on the floor as I watched him dress for his date. I asked him if I meant anything to him. Honestly, I don't recall an answer from him. I begged him to please spend some time with me, but my pleas fell on deaf ears.

I stared hopelessly, wanting some ray of hope from MY HUS-BAND! I suppose God himself must have stopped me from grabbing him around the knees and begging him to just talk to me. Knowing that he was leaving very soon for his date, I asked him a question that I hate to share with you. I said, "Can I at least be one of your girlfriends since you don't want me as a wife now?" I didn't ask to be his only girlfriend; I asked to be one of them. How sad to realize that a piece of molded crumbs would be sufficient for me! He looked at me cruelly and said, "I'll think about it." It is even sadder that I felt a sigh of relief. He said he would at least think about it and, to me, that was better than no.

He hurried me out of his apartment and walked ahead of me. He got into his car and left before I did. I could hear the demons laughing at me. I could also feel his desire for me to follow him so that he could further humiliate me. Thank God, I took my wounded, pitiful self home. Of all the pain and torment, this was the worst for me. I sought the Lord, with bitter tears, to please stop me from pleading for crumbs. After a short period of time, the Lord did help me to hold my peace. The desperate feelings remained, but God enabled me to stop begging him to throw me a bone.

Still More Torment

The boys began school in a new environment and I began a new job. I worked with individuals with all types of disabilities, but the environment was not as tormenting to me. At least, not in the beginning. I continued to struggle with my sanity. I did have a doctor who I truly liked. He explained things thoroughly in reference to the medication. At one point though, I just quit taking the anti-depressants. I knew that I wasn't depressed. I didn't need anyone to tell me that I was anymore. I was tormented. There was something sitting on my shoulders, pressing on my head and I couldn't make it stop.

I was sitting in the office talking to the secretary when, all of a sudden, she began to fade away from my eyesight. I could hear her talking to me, but I could no longer see her. I began to panic on the inside and the Lord said, "Just keep talking." I knew if I reacted, she would freak out and I would end up in the hospital. I knew that if I went back, I would die. I know at times that I did want to die, but not like that. She finally reappeared and I made an excuse to get out of there. I found somewhere to cry. I cried so much. I knew that I wasn't depressed but what was this. I knew that it was a spiritual battle, but for what?

I learned how to live with my constant torment outside of my home. However, when I got home I barely had the strength to take care of my children. I tried to pretend that I was okay when I was around my boys.

One Saturday morning, I just laid in bed, afraid to get up. I knew what would face me and I was so tired. My oldest son, who was about eight at the time, came into my room with a plate of food. He said, "I made you breakfast, Momma, please eat." I had gone from a size twelve to a size seven. I sat up in the bed and saw that he had really worked hard to fix something for me to eat. Needless to say, he had never cooked anything in his life. He had some very-well-cooked eggs along with thoroughly fried wieners, toast and biscuits. I begged God to please help me to eat it. I wanted to do it for him. It took me about an hour, but I forced it down. I didn't want them to worry about me. They had their own struggles, dealing with their father being gone. He seldom came by to get them, and the older two really missed him. They prayed all of the time for him to come back to us and be the way he used to be.

No Hope in Sight

I wanted church to be to me what I knew it could be, but the harder I tried to seek God, the more the demons would press upon me. I watched others apply the Word and get help, but when I would bind the devil, I got worse. When I would testify about God's goodness—well, it's hard to explain, but I would get beat up. The more I prayed for myself, the worse I would get. Actually, everything seemed to get worse when I prayed fervently. Most of the time, I would find a quiet place and just sit still. I would try not to think or pray. I learned to be still when the torment was at its worst. There were certain times that I could listen to music, but I had to be careful what I listened to. For the most part, I could only listen to songs of worship. The torment would briefly subside when worship was played. I understand why Saul needed David to play the harp for him. I Samuel 16:23 reads:

> *And it came to pass, when the evil spirit from God was upon Saul, that David took an harp, and played with his hand: so Saul was refreshed, and was well, and the evil spirit departed from him.*

Calm refreshing worship music such as "Praise Strings," and the like, was always very comforting to me. Demons can't stand for us to worship God. There were certain gospel artists I could not listen to because the torment would worsen for me when I did. I realize there are those who like to drag those we consider depressed to various musicals and concerts. Watch closely and you will notice that the person may become more restless and uneasy. We have assumed that it's because the songs are anointed and the demons don't want to hear it. We especially get confused if everyone around is supposedly "praising God." I am not talking about someone who is struggling with self pity, I am talking about those held captive by Satan's assassins. Yes, I know that there are times when the person needs to shake themselves and not let the devil ride. However, that is not always the solution, and all music is not God-ordained, regardless of how good it sounds. Music ordained by God has the power to bring deliverance, healing and encouragement, not just a good feeling to replace our years on the dance floor. Music should not just stir up our flesh and emotions, it should minister to us like a Balm in Gilead. *Amen!*

My home became a refuge for me. I would hibernate. I was weary of facing the world, so any chance I could get I would just stay inside. I would seldom answer my door. I really didn't want a lot of visitors. I was content with occasional visits from Jacque. I trusted her. She understood me and never made me feel crazy. One evening, there was a knock on the door. It was the sheriff. I remember my heart sinking as he handed me some papers. In my heart I said to God, "Why, are you letting him divorce me? Why wouldn't you let me divorce him?" As I opened the paper it wasn't a petition for divorce, it was a foreclosure on the house. The pain was different from how I felt initially, however it was still painful. Now, the whole town could see my home repossessed. So much humiliation. So much trouble. The song "Trouble in my way" became my motto.

With no relief, I had given up. The more I prayed the worse things would get for me. I know this sounds horrible. but at times it was better for me when I didn't pray, so I began to ask God to let us die in our sleep. I didn't want to live and I didn't want to leave my children. I asked him to take us all. Each morning as I was blessed with a new day, I was angry. God would hardly answer anything for me.

Overlooking the Blessing

Through my torment, I realized that I was overlooking something: the gift of discerning of spirits. The torment was the same, but I was beginning to recognize some things. When I was around certain people, the oppression would be unbearable. Please understand, this gift is not as glorious as I thought it would be. I never got a good feeling when the Lord allowed the gift to operate and, let me assure you, it only operates as the Lord allows. I do not walk around judging people, neither do I broadcast what I feel as the gift operates. Even today, as the Spirit of the Lord allows the gift to operate I don't feel a glory cloud. Very often, I can feel the oppression on a person or the pain they feel. I have gone into places and felt the power ruling and could only pray and not say a word. I suppose the Father had to see if he could trust me with such a gift. I know that initially I wanted this gift for my glory—not for His glory, and divine purpose.

I recall one particular Sunday, an Evangelist came through town and sat in on our Sunday School. He knew a lot of the Word and he shared things with us that we had previously discussed in class. However, I knew that something was wrong because the oppression tightened on my head. I was not the pastor and it was not right to become the church busybody so I prayed. He remained for church and participated in the praise service. I knew what was happening to me, but I had to keep it to myself and continue to pray. He began to minister to certain individuals in the congregation. The oppression intensified and I kept praying. At one point, I looked up at Pastor Harris. When our eyes met I knew that God had revealed it to her as well. She graciously retrieved the microphone and took back what the enemy was trying to do. Later, I was informed about some ungodly things the evangelist was participating in. All I had been required to do was pray.

I began to discern God's voice, my voice, and Satan's voice. Many times I would sit on my couch and hear things. I found myself from time to time saying, "God I know that's not you, that's me."

Even though I couldn't pray like I wanted to, fast like I wanted to, read like I wanted to, I learned that I could listen. So, I tried as often as I could to just listen. I knew when it was Satan or his imps trying to drive me crazy, or my own self doing the same. I learned to be cautious and not open myself up to a person just because they say they are a Christian. Truthfully, even today, because of my experiences I am more guarded than most. I have paid a tremendous price for my lack of wisdom.

After a while, the torment didn't last all day every day. The Lord would sometimes give me a couple of hours of the day (mostly evening) when he made the powers leave me alone. I could read a couple of scriptures or talk to a friend without complaining about my trial. I was always in pain about my marriage. I couldn't divorce him and he wouldn't divorce me. He was playing the field and I was helpless. Different people would tell me who he was with and what they were doing. One friend of mine told me something that helped. I told her the things that I was being told and she said, "Sister Doll, tell those people that you are not a garbage can and stop bringing you trash."

The pastors asked me to teach Sunday School. I wanted to accept, but I was concerned about the pressure to study. I was only able to read a little of the Word, how could I be effective? No matter how difficult it was for me to study, each Sunday morning God blessed. I was amazed.

The Spirit of God began to pull out of me the Word that I had stored up years ago. I learned that we have to store up the Word in our hearts when things are going well. From my own experience, I've learned that if I hadn't searched the scriptures, studied the word and hid it in my heart those first few years, things would have been worse for me. If I had not put anything in, nothing would come out.

God Please Stop Me!

The outer torment, coupled with the inner pain, seemed to be more and more unbearable. I was taking my youngest son to a school function when I saw my husband with another woman. It was early one afternoon and it was very apparent to me that he hadn't been to work that day. He had on shorts and no shirt. They were leaving his apartment. Apparently, I was a glutton for pain. I pulled up and called his name. Even the presence of our son didn't deter him from openly humiliating me. I walked into that punishment, but I couldn't help myself. I listened to his words of cruelty as I watched the smirk on her face. It was also apparent from the look on her face that she felt like this was her man. He was my husband, yet I had no rights, no say-so, nothing.

It was a constant experience for me to see him with other women. I was five years his senior and one of the women was five years my senior. I knew this woman from church. She would visit Pastor Boyd's church on evangelistic night and I thought that would matter. I was so naïve and confused. I suppose their relationship hurt me the most. It was obvious to me that she had a lot more to offer him financially. She had her own business and he frequently drove her new car. The Lord continued to tell me, no divorce. This didn't make any sense to me.

There was no relief from the oppression. I wanted this to be over. I needed it to be over. I needed some relief but couldn't find any. So, I looked for something to make me feel better. Actually, I looked for someone to make me feel better. I remembered a nice man who had befriended me when I worked for the Mental Health agency. I obtained his phone number and I called him. Yes, I called him. I still remember the first question I asked him. After he rec- ognized who I was, I asked him if he had a girlfriend or a wife. He laughed and said, "No woman has ever asked that question right off the bat." We talked, and he asked if he could come by some-time. Of course, that was what I wanted (so I thought).

He eventually came by. We talked and he interacted well with my children which pleased me. He continually complimented me, telling me every lie that I wanted to hear. Eventually it led to the ultimate fall. I had put myself in a position to compromise. Remember, at that time I didn't realize that I was desperate for the covering God had given me. This part of me I had hoped was long gone, but it wasn't. Without the covering, I had become easy prey for the enemy.

I didn't receive what I needed. I simply added to my pain. Now, I had fallen and was condemned. The enemy told me that I was a hypocrite. He told me that I had to give up and stop going to church. How could I? The church was the only place where I received temporary relief.

The following Sunday, I was not concerned about the opinion of the people, I had to confess. I wanted to please God. I had already lost just about everything, so what else could happen? People would talk about me? Too late for that, they already were. I was already labeled a fool. I wanted to rid myself of the guilt, so I confessed openly. I told the church I had fallen. If they judged me, it didn't show. Most were surprised that I had the courage to openly confess my sin.

I asked Pastor Rudy Harris to pray for me. I whispered my request in his ear as he gave the church the opportunity for prayer. Immediately, he looked up and said to the congregation, "I have never heard such a request from anyone. Sister Doll, asked for me to agree in prayer with her that her yes to God would be yes." I no longer wanted my "yes" to God to be "yes" only when I felt like saying "yes." I couldn't trust much that I felt anyway. I needed my "yes" to be "yes" to God when I was in pain. I did not want it just to be lip service. I wanted to mean "yes" even though it had taken me to the cross.

Tempted Again

The yearning to be loved was ever present. Every kind gesture between a husband and wife that I witnessed was like a dagger in my heart. That was the part I strongly disliked about going to church. As I watched the couples at church interact with one another, each act of kindness was personified. I would fight the tears, and question what I had done so wrong to deserve this pain. I longed for my sons to have their godly father again, and I wanted a husband - my husband.

One of the other sisters in the church was also separated from her husband and we often talked to one another. We understood what others didn't about our pain. We prayed together, laughed together, and tried to keep each other encouraged. In spite of my torment, different people would lean on me for strength, though I barely had the strength to hold myself up. Each time I helped someone, the Lord would remind me that His grace was sufficient. I received a call one night from Sister Dobie. She told me that she and her husband were discussing a reconciliation. I was happy for her, but sad for myself. She had not been separated as long as I had and now it appeared that God was moving for her and not for me.

As we continued to talk, she said something that blessed my soul. She said, "Sister Doll, you have gone through a lot for longer than I have and you deserve your family to be restored." She then said, "I don't want to reconcile with my husband until God works out your relationship with your husband." I had never heard such unselfishness in my life, but I had to tell her what the Lord was speaking to me. I told Sister Dobie that her ministry was not my ministry, and her tests were not mine. I let her know that God was in control, and the enemy of her soul would perhaps tempt her in an area that God was restoring to give her a way of escape. I let her know that it was her time and obviously was not mine. God how that hurt, but I knew it was the right thing.

Very soon after our conversation, she and her husband reunited. I was so blessed and encouraged for her, but it added to my pain. I couldn't talk to anyone about this because I didn't want to appear jealous. I wasn't jealous, I was in pain.

The enemy of my soul knew the pain I was going through so, once again, I had a visit from the guy I had fallen with. He came by one evening and we watched television. All of my sons had gone to sleep and we began to talk. The battle within began to rage. I wanted to be loved so badly, and though I knew he didn't love me, I wanted him to. The Lord began to speak to me about my commitment to him. I wanted to override that voice but I couldn't, I wouldn't. I asked my friend if he would do me a favor. He looked at me and said, "If I can."

I asked, "When you walk out of the door, will you walk out of my life?" I will never forget his response all the days of my life.

He sternly looked me in the eye and said, "No problem. It will be like I never knew you." With those words he walked out the door and never looked back. I felt like my heart was on fire. I cried, and cried. It was not supposed to happen this way. A short time later, he began to date the woman whose duplex was adjoined to mine.

More Defeat

Many people continued to come to me to talk about their problems and for me to pray for them. Couldn't they understand that I couldn't help myself? Couldn't they see that I was slowly dying and gradually losing every bit of my mind? These people would leave encouraged and blessed, and I couldn't get a prayer through for myself. To further complicate things, each time God used me to help someone, well, it's really hard to explain. The only way I can describe this is: I would get beat up. Something would happen to make the pressures on me clamp down even tighter. The more I obeyed God, the more torment I experienced. Most of the time I had to wrestle with myself to obey God. Each act of obedience for me came with a price. Even following instructions given to the church presented penalties for me.

Thank God, Pastor Jacque understood. She would call me and give me separate instructions at times, because she recognized the extra price I would pay for following the instructions to the letter. If the church was instructed to go on a three day fast, my instructions would be similar to what the pregnant women were to do. I struggled to eat anyway, so the enemy looked for any opportunity to end my life.

There remained no visual change in sight for my husband. One afternoon, as I went to visit my sons at the pastor's home, my husband stopped by. I was on my lunch hour and he saw my car. He came by to get me to sign some loan papers. He was in need of money to consolidate some bills and he assured me that he would give me a portion of the money. He knew the financial struggle I was having. Needless to say, he needed my signature for the loan approval. However, I didn't receive one single dime. What a fool I was!

Not long afterwards, he came to me and said he was filing bankruptcy. We had been that route before. Seven years before, to be exact. What was he thinking? Didn't he remember what we went through? Didn't he remember how humiliating it was to need basic things in life and have bad credit? That didn't matter to him. He was looking for another easy way out. Even through my torment, I knew this was wrong. I resisted, only to find out all of the marital debt would fall on me. My attorney told me that I didn't have a choice. "GOD, where are you?" I thought, "why is all of this happening to me?" My life had little to no meaning whatsoever.

I signed the bankruptcy papers. My husband was released from all previous debt and I came away with my car. I needed the transportation, so I resigned the note agreeing to continue with my obligation. I didn't get a thank you from my husband. I sought the Lord with bitter tears, but God continued to say, "No divorce. My Grace is sufficient for you."

As the torment continued, my mind and emotions seemed to worsen. Strangely enough, I could even feel when my husband was going to call or come by. A strong demonic power would come over me seconds before he would call me. He would call, sometimes, in the evening when I got home from work and curse me unmercifully. He constantly badgered me for not being a good mother or for not consulting him on a decision about the boys. I would hold the phone trembling. When he would finish and hang up, seconds later that demonic power would lift. Once again I begged God, only to hear, "My grace is sufficient for you."

My pastors prayed and even Pastor Rudy became frustrated and weary with my husband's behaviors. He believed that I should divorce him. I had biblical grounds to do this. My husband was in open adultery and didn't care what anyone thought. Pastor Jacque never wavered. She always said, "What did the Lord say?"

My sons suffered terribly. Their father would have them around his various women and they became confused by what they saw. They would tell me things the women would say to them and the different things that transpired. They hated it. I had to help them with their pain while trying not to show mine.

Late at night, or should I say early in the mornings (around 1:00 or 2:00 am), my telephone would sometimes ring. It would always be my husband. He would say, in a very soft voice, "Doll, I love you." He would immediately hang up. I never responded. In a way, those phone calls gave a momentary relief, but shortly thereafter they also added to my mind battles.

A Small Glimmer of Insight

A few months after our separation, a young lady was hired at the agency I was employed with. When I introduced myself to her, she recognized my last name and asked if I was related to a former classmate of hers. She named my husband. Small world. She told me she had seen him at the high school reunion and described how much fun they had. She said she had some pictures she would like to show me. She began to laugh and say, "He was hypnotized at the reunion." She described the things he had done while under hypnosis. I couldn't believe what she was saying.

She brought the pictures in and I was so grieved seeing how he had performed under hypnosis. She laughed hysterically about all of the fun they had watching him (basically, he made a fool of himself). I couldn't believe that he could submit his mind and will to be hypnotized. How could he open a door that wide for the enemy? At that time I didn't know much about hypnosis, but I knew enough to know that it was not of God.

This woman's information brought a little insight. It explained a conversation my husband and I had recently had. One evening, he had come by to see the boys while I was folding clothes. He came over to where I was and asked if he could talk to me. I said "yes" only because I was afraid to say "no." I didn't want any conflict, so I pretended to be interested in what he had to say. He wanted to talk to me about one of his women. He began to talk about the older woman, saying he felt trapped in the relationship. Excuse me, but did I become invisible? He acted as if I wasn't his wife. He said she made him feel like he needed her and he felt like he couldn't get out of the relationship. I looked at him in amazement as I thought, "Well, you didn't have any problem getting out of a marriage with three sons!" It was a bizarre moment.

He continued to talk as if he desperately needed me to give him a solution. I could hear the demons that tormented me, laughing. The spiritual battle was so hard. I could hear the Holy Spirit saying to hold my peace. The Lord wasn't just instructing me to be quiet, he was literally saying, "Hold your peace." Hold onto what little peace you have. This was a setup up to send me over the edge. Often, Satan will use his assassins to attack your mind and emotions to send you over the edge.

I literally had to hold on. I was on a roller coaster ride against my will. I have learned why it is so important to literally do as Ephesians 6:11-17 instructs, which tells God's soldiers to:

> *Put on God's whole armor (the armor of a heavy-armed soldier which God supplies), that you may be able successfully to stand up against (all) the strategies and deceits of the devil.*
>
> *For we wrestle not with flesh and blood (contending only with physical opponents), but against the*

despotisms, against the powers, against (the master spirits who are) the world rulers of this present darkness, against the spirit forces of wickedness in the heavenly (supernatural) sphere

Therefore put on God's complete armor, that you may be able to resist and stand your ground on the evil day (of danger) and, having done all (the crisis demands) to stand (firmly in your place)

Stand therefore (hold your ground), having tightened the belt of truth around your loins and having put on the breastplate of integrity and moral rectitude and right standing with God.

And having shod your feet in preparation (to face the enemy with the firm-footed stability, the promptness, and readiness produced by the good news) of the Gospel of peace.

Lift up over all the (covering) shield of saving faith, upon which you can quench all the flaming missiles of the wicked (one).

And take the helmet of salvation and the sword that the Spirit wields which is the Word of God

I never said a word. I just stared at him. I needed the armor just to stand. I needed the armor just to resist the power sent to attack an already wounded soldier. I recall one Sunday night at church, I went before the congregation and attempted to explain my desperate need for the saints to continue in intensive prayer for me. I could tell by the look on many of the faces that they had no clue, and I repeat, no clue about the battles I encountered on a daily basis. I remember pleading with them to help me in prayer. I begged them not to let another wounded soldier die. Day in and day out, I would listen to the song by: Reba Rambo and Dony McGuire, "Wounded Soldier." The words would play over and over in my head: *underlined or italicized*

> See all the wounded; Hear all their desperate cries for help
> Pleading for shelter and for peace, Our comrades are suf-
> fering
> Come let us meet them at their need, Don't let a wounded
> soldier die
>
> (Chorus)
> Come let us pour the oil, come let us bind the hurt,
> let's cover them with the blanket of his love.
> Come let us break the bread, come let us give them rest.
> Let's minister healing to them, please, don't let another
> wounded soldier, DIE.
>
> Obeying their orders, They fought on the front lines for
> our King
> Capturing the enemy's stronghold, Weakened from battle
> Satan crept in to steal their lives, Don't let another
> wounded soldier die
>
> 1985 New Kingdom Music

The next thing was even more strange: My husband fell asleep. He said what he had to say and went right to sleep. I did awaken him later and he did not mention the conversation, so neither did I. I truly believe he had no remembrance of the previous conversation.

Trouble on the Highway

During the summer months, our agency received a contract to provide employment services for youth in the surrounding counties. We hired two instructors and it was my responsibility to monitor classroom instruction throughout the county. This meant a lot of traveling for me, but I looked forward to getting out of the office. I handled the torment better sometimes when I was alone. It would give me the opportunity to talk to God alone, and to listen to my music. I had one particular tape that ministered to me and I played it repeatedly.

My first trip worried me. As I drove down the highway, I became extremely sleepy. I turned up my music, put the air conditioner on full blast and even tried to sing. Nothing was working. I tried slapping myself. From time to time, something would jolt me just as I would begin to cross the center line. I prayed and prayed for God to help me stay awake. It didn't help to pull to the shoulder and stop because as soon as I got back in the car it would begin again.

I was grateful to make it to my destination. I purchased sodas, just for the caffeine, but to no avail. There was something that rode with me. I dreaded the trip back. I hoped it was just me, but on the trip home the [same]? exact thing happened.

Each trip presented the same trial. I would begin the trip with tears in my eyes as I asked God to please get me to my destination safely. I always made it, but I would have the exact same experience. I thought of all the times that I prayed to die and was upset because the Lord didn't allow it. Now, Satan was trying to kill me and I didn't want to die, at least not this way. Only the grace of God carried me through those experiences that summer.

Vengeance Belongs to God

I distanced myself from my precious co-workers at the Mental Health. I hated the stares from those who had known me when I was well. On many occasions, individuals would say to me, "Where's the old Doll?" Why did they say that to me? I wanted her back more than anything. [or anyone] I had reconciled myself to the fact that I may never find her again. Perhaps, if my path crossed the agent of Satan from the conference, I could get her back. There was never a chance that would happen.

One afternoon, I received a call from my former supervisor (the one who took me to the conference). We exchanged pleasant greetings and I hoped she wouldn't ask me if I were any better. I didn't want to explain something that I didn't understand myself. She did inquire about my struggle and I assured her that I was all right. With that she got to the reason for the call.

She stated, "I interviewed a young lady who used you as a character reference for employment." She then gave the name of the lady I had at one time considered as my daughter. I couldn't believe it! The same young woman who was cooking at my home? She had used me for a reference. Why, the unmitigated gall! I gripped the receiver tightly. I felt this was my opportunity to tell all. I knew my former supervisor would adhere to my recommendation. Then I heard a voice deep within say, "Vengeance is Mine, I will repay." As I gasped for breath I said, " She is a very nice person, give her an opportunity."

I must have held the receiver for a long time after she hung up. I felt like I was driving the nails into my own coffin. I began to understand that neither my pain, nor another person's behavior, exempted me from obeying the truth. The truth of the Word of God burned deep within my being. The word says, in Romans 12:17-21;

Repay no man evil for evil, but take thought for what is honest and proper and noble (aiming to be above reproach) in the sight of everyone.

If it be possible, as far as it depends on you, live at peace with everyone.

Beloved, never avenge yourselves, but leave the way open for (God's) wrath; for it is written, Vengeance is Mine, I will repay (requite), says the Lord.

But if your enemy is hungry, feed him; if he is thirsty, give him drink; for by doing so you will heap burning coals upon his head.

Do not let yourself be overcome with evil, but overcome (master) evil with good. Amplified Version

The Road to Freedom

God had given me favor with my present supervisor. He had just purchased a home and encouraged me also to pursue buying a house. I didn't have the nerve to tell him that I had to walk away from the house God had given me. That house was located on a main street so, from time to time, I had to pass it on my travels. I hated looking at it. There was a big (big to me) HUD sign in the front yard, so it was obvious to everyone that there had been a foreclosure on this house. Every single time I passed that house, I would tell the Lord how sorry I was for not being able to keep his blessing. I knew I wasn't solely responsible, but it still hurt and I still felt like a failure.

My supervisor continued to pressure me, so to appease him I called a Realtor. I didn't know what I was doing, but I felt compelled to follow his suggestions. When I met with the Realtor I was very upfront about my financial situation. At one point I thought, "what are you doing? You can't buy a house with a foreclosure on another." We drove around and looked at a few houses. He assured me that it was not impossible to get a house. He did say it might be difficult and I wasn't pressured to get a house. I had a nice place to live that God had provided.

After we had looked at what I thought was our last house, he quickly said, "Let me show you a house on 12th Street." I asked him the address and he said, "320 N. 12th."

"No way am I going to that house," I quickly replied. He was insistent and I was in pain. My boys were with me and as we pulled up in the driveway, tears flooded my eyes. When we entered the door, I felt like God was letting the enemy play a cruel and dirty trick on me. It was just like we had left it. It had been a year and no one had lived in it since we left. My boys were excited just to be there. They had so many good memories and so did I. I couldn't afford it then, and sure couldn't afford it now. And what about my credit?

I called my brother on the Realtor's cellular phone to ask him for advice. He has always been a whiz with ideas and I knew he would give me sound advice. I told him where I was and asked him what, if anything, could I do? He asked me to put the Realtor on the phone. He asked the realtor, "What do I need to do to get my sister back in her house?" I couldn't believe it. He was my only living brother but we had never been that close. What was God doing? The Realtor informed him he would need $500.00 to take it off the market and then the process could begin. Needless to say, no one else had put an offer on the house. God sovereignly moved and gave me my house back! He not only gave it back to me, but the payments were half of what we were initially paying. Also, the first note had been for thirty years and the second one was for only fifteen years. Praise God!

The torment still remained, but I had hope! God wasn't finished yet. Sometime earlier, the boys and I were at church as usual and my husband walked in. I couldn't believe it. After the Word was preached, Pastor Rudy Harris called him up for prayer. God began to minister to the deep wounds in his soul. He didn't immediately change (actually, at times, he seemed worse) but eventually God began to answer my children's prayers. I couldn't see it, or maybe I didn't want to. So much had happened, so much pain. I didn't tell him about the house initially, as he was coming around more. At times, I saw glimpses of the man I married. Only glimpses. Sin had taken a toll and he wasn't standing as tall as he used to. He talked of getting his family back. I wanted that, but I was afraid and I wasn't yet free from the oppression.

I went to my Pastors for counseling. Pastor Jacque always had the same stand. She had sought the Lord with me about my marriage and God said no divorce. Even though many times during the separation God allowed the enemy to use my husband to inflict more pain on me, Pastor Jacque never changed her stand. No matter what happened she would always say, "Sister Doll, but what did the Lord say?" She confessed, in church, that she personally wanted to avenge me of my adversary, but she chose to obey God.

When I told her about getting the house back, she told me that my husband was coming home. I didn't see it. He and I didn't talk about it and I was afraid to believe.

He moved us in just like he had moved us out. We moved in without him, but early one Sunday morning, despite the fact that there was deep, deep snow on the ground, there was a knock at the door. It was him and I was surprised. He came in with his head down. I really wasn't ready to hear what he was going to say, but he said he was sorry and he really wanted his family back. He wanted to come home. I had learned the voice of God through my trial and I knew my voice as well. The torment was with me for fewer hours of the day. Some days if I could make it until 12:00 noon, it would lift. I heard the Lord say "okay," so I told my husband "okay." Just like that. The boys were happy, but we were guarded because there was a lot of pain to overcome.

Just When I Thought It Was Over

He moved out of his apartment and we re-established our home. Five days after he moved in, he was terminated from his job. Not laid off, terminated. He quickly began to reap what he had sown, but I couldn't understand why it had to affect all of us. He fought depression daily. He filed a lawsuit with EEOC. He had to start over. He began to look for a job, but he could only find temporary work. For whatever the reason (I guess you can blame it on the depression), once again the boys and I were going to church without him. I had to keep my relationship with God. I had been confused before and I knew where this road would lead me.

It was hard to continue to fight through the oppression, to deal with his depression, with my family and with all the fiery darts from others. Now, to top it off, the Father was telling me to walk in love. What? When is someone going to care about my feelings?

My husband was so depressed that he would sit glued to a chair in front of the television. One Sunday night after church, I found him in his usual chair and I was angry because I was once again taking our sons to church Sunday morning and night by myself. As I entered the door, the Holy Spirit said, "Ask him if he wants something to eat." I tried to resist but I gave in. When I asked him he said, "Sure honey." This wasn't fair. I had cooked, so the least he could do was fix his own plate. Besides, why wasn't he asking to fix my plate? I reluctantly obeyed and dragged my wounded self upstairs. After I had settled in, the Holy Spirit said, "Ask him if he wants seconds."

I finally did and he said, as he handed me his plate, "Thank you, baby, I sure do." I fixed his plate and crawled back up the stairs with tears streaming down my face.

A few months after we had moved back into the house, he announced he was leaving. He was moving to Delaware because he couldn't get on his feet. I was floored. I didn't think he was really serious, but he packed his car and left during the night.

Now, I was not only tormented, I was bitter. I began to question if I had really heard God. After all, I still fought the torment day after day. God surely would not have had me take my husband back knowing that he would eventually leave us again. This can't be God. I still didn't have the answer to my torment. I couldn't keep going through these trials. I didn't feel like I was totally stable yet, anyway. I had not only taken myself off the anti-depressants but I had reduced my dosage of anti-anxiety medication. No one other than Pastor Jacque knew about my medicine. The church was still condemning such things. They still considered it a lack of faith to take them. From time to time, I bitterly struggled with taking it at all. I knew God could heal me. I believed he could. Some days I fought my way through without any, to prove to myself I could make it. I needed to know that I wasn't dependent on it. The Holy Ghost so gently spoke to me and said, "Human bodies and emotions are not built to take the kind of pressure you are under." He further said, "You are going to have an extensive healing process to restore you, take the medicine." I had cut myself back to one a day. Although the Holy Spirit had spoken to me, I continued to struggle when I listened to ministers that I respected preach against it. It has taken me a very long time to walk in victory in that area.

Another Test

If my tests were open book ones, I was studying the wrong chapters. I received a call from a Vocational Rehabilitation Counselor, who presented me with another challenge. I frequently received calls from that agency because they were responsible for referring individuals to our agency for training. This counselor and I were on a first name basis. He called to refer a client, but told me that he was unsure if the individual would follow through with the vocational plan developed. The potential clients' mother had a difficult time when she realized who she needed to call for assistance. There were basically no other options, at that time, in the city in which we lived. Our agency provided the needed services and I was the contact person. Guess who the client's mother was? The very woman I had grieved the most over regarding her relationship with my husband. WHY LORD, WHY?

Once again, I did not believe I had the strength to face this woman. I couldn't imagine finding the courage to endure a meeting with her. Working with her daughter was not a problem for me, as I had met her, years before, when they visited our church. I was fond of her daughter from our prior meeting and I had some understanding of her needs.

The Lord did give me a little time, as the mother didn't call me for a few weeks. One Friday morning, I received a call from her. The day I dreaded had come. I scheduled an appointment with her for the following Monday.

I prayed for strength all weekend. In spite of what I had to face on Monday, life didn't stop happening that weekend just because I had to face my giant in three days. The torment, pain, loss of appetite, and struggles with my inability to focus remained. My prayers only resulted in the same familiar answer from God: "My grace is sufficient." *outside of quotes*

She arrived promptly on Monday morning. I could see the strain in her eyes when we faced one another. God's grace prevailed as I explained our program; gave her a tour; and completed the necessary paperwork. She explained how to care for her daughter should any problems arise. We must have spent over an hour together. I gave her a start date for her daughter and I was still alive at the end of the meeting.

Her daughter and I immediately developed a strong bond and I grew very fond of her. On Valentine's day, she admired the cards I had received and wanted to get her mother something. I suggested that we make her a card on the computer. At that particular time, she had limited reading ability so I typed what I believed were the sentiments of her heart for her mother. As I read it to her, she smiled and gave me a big hug.

On a few occasions, this young lady would need to return home before her scheduled time to leave. On one occasion I called her mother to pick her up. She was unable to leave her place of business at the time of the call and though she did attempt to find someone to provide the necessary transportation for her daughter, she wasn't successful. When she called back, she apologized and said it would be a while before she could get there. There was a brief silence. I knew she needed my assistance, so I offered to take her daughter home. She graciously thanked me and I assured her that I would not enter her home, but would wait in the car to return her daughter to training. She asked me to please feel welcomed to come into her home.

Her daughter was excited that we were going together. It was a very long and apprehensive drive for me. How would I feel as I entered the place my husband had visited so many times? The pain and anxiety seemed to suffocate my heart. "God, how many more tests?" I pulled up to a very nice home and the daughter invited me in. I sat, silently waiting and talking to God. I remember thinking, "God, what are you doing?" This situation happened at least two other times before I realized that this, too, was part of a process that I didn't understand at that time. To my amazement, each visit gradually got easier.

Please Stop Testing Me

My husband called frequently, but I still couldn't understand why he left like he did. Why did he get to run? It wasn't fair. Months passed. He wanted me to visit, but I refused. Finally, about 5 months later I visited Delaware. He was excited. I was angry. I wanted him to help me find the answer to my torment, which had now lasted for over 6 years. No one wanted to talk about it and honestly, I didn't either, but I needed an answer. My husband wanted to take me to see the city. I hated it. As he drove down I-95 the Lord said, "Move."

"God, no! Please, don't do this to me."

Again he said, "Move." I had made a lot of vows to God during my torment. I had promised him that I would do whatever he wanted me to if he would just lift the torment.

Moving to Delaware would mean that I would be alone. My husband had an older brother and sister there, but I didn't know them that well. Pastor Jacque would not be close enough to help me. I knew we could keep in touch but what would I do if I really needed her? Many times, she would appear on my doorstep when I was in a crisis. Why would God want me to start over? I was still tormented and I didn't know why. This trial had lasted more than six years. I didn't believe I could carry this torment to another state and endure alone.

I wanted to please the Father, even though for the past few years I didn't know what he was doing. I knew that I had missed God's instructions many times, so maybe I wasn't hearing well this time. Who was I fooling? I knew it was God. He didn't give me a long dissertation about why he wanted me to move. He spoke firmly, as a Father would speak to a child who would try to reason with him. He firmly spoke one word, "Move."

School ended for summer break. I only told a few people because I knew that they would try to talk me out of it and I would have let them. During my visit earlier, I interviewed with the same company in Delaware that employed me at home. When I moved to Delaware, I was hired doing basically the same job I did at home. The change was hard for me. I had no family, no friends, and no church.

I felt alone. I couldn't go to a doctor and explain what I had been through; yet now, the torment seemed to last a little longer. I also had to face a real highway to get to work: Interstate 95. There were no major crowded highways in my hometown. The majority of the roads I had traveled on were two lanes. Occasionally there were four lanes but never ten! I was tormented and petrified.

I recalled the enemy's attempt to kill me on the road in Oklahoma so I knew what I might face. At times, it seemed as though that power greeted me as I started my day on the road. My supervisor would allow me to leave early to avoid the heavier, rush hour traffic. I would cry as the power would engulf me. As I reached out to God, I discovered his words never changed even though I was a long way from home. He continued to speak the familiar scripture, "My grace is sufficient for thee." The only other scripture he would lead me to, throughout my years of testing, was I Peter 5:10, which reads:

> But the God of all grace, who hath called us unto his eternal glory by Christ Jesus, after that ye have suffered awhile, make you perfect, stablish, strengthened, settle you.

I had hoped that my move to Delaware was going to be the end of the torment. I had convinced myself that was why God wanted me to move. It was somewhat good for my marriage. My children were happy that we were a family again and my husband seemed to be really trying to make the marriage work.

He had joined a particular church prior to our move. He even joined the choir. He felt this would help me settle in more in Delaware. Knowing I had continued my walk with God, he thought this would help me to like this new state better.

I tried to enjoy his church. I really tried. When things happened contrary to the Word as we had come to know it, he would just look at me, smile and say, "Doll, don't say nothing." He knew better, but was content with the compromise. The boys even knew something wasn't right. They would say to me, "Mama, we don't like that church, it's so dead." I didn't last long there. I couldn't afford to compromise at this stage. I knew Satan would use anything to push me over the edge. I was more tormented in the church than I was outside of it.

Where Do We Go?

The boys and I pursued another place to fellowship. Even though my husband stopped going to the other church at the same time we did, he didn't help us look for another place to fellowship, so we searched alone.

I asked God to please lead me because I was afraid not to be in fellowship. I prayed and searched. Then, I visited a very nice place where I enjoyed the Praise and Worship, but, for some reason, I could never settle in.

The Lord kept speaking to me about starting my own fellowship. I thought, "Well, that's strange. I didn't really know anyone except a few people at my job and my immediate family. How was God expecting a tormented, dislocated woman with a backslidden husband to start a fellowship?

After a little while, a lady at work (that God was using me to minister to) asked me to please start a bible study. God had always used me to encourage others, and to minister to others, in spite of my struggle to stay sane. Actually, the only time the torment would lift was when I was witnessing and sharing the Word of God with others.

I started the Bible study, initially, with my husband and one lady from work. I was so blessed and encouraged that he wanted to participate. As we searched the scriptures together again, it seemed like old times. My vision for his ministry, our ministry, was being revived.

I thought this was all that I needed for the torment to end. I had told myself many times, "When my husband comes back to God and takes his rightful place, I'll get free." I had stopped talking to him about my torment, years before because he couldn't deal with it. Besides that, he used to tell me how weak I was, and since I couldn't bear hearing that all of the time, he didn't know how much I continued to battle.

I had convinced myself of a lie. The torment didn't stop. My husband's participation in the Bible study didn't change my trial one single bit. I was so confused and miserable. Everything I had thought I needed to be free was just my restless anticipation. I continued to pray for people and watched God miraculously heal and deliver. The mother of one of my co-workers was critically ill. Vernita was frantic with fear that her mother was dying. She called me from the hospital and told me the doctor was unable to feel her mother's pulse, and her blood pressure was extremely low. She asked me to come to the hospital and pray for her mother. Why me? Where was her pastor?

I couldn't say no, but God knows I wanted to. As I entered the hospital, the powers pressed heavily upon my head. Pain entered my heart as I saw the emergency room. I hadn't been to a medical hospital since my mother had died and my heart was aching and my head spinning. I wanted to run. I could feel death. I could feel the plots of the enemy being carried out on hopeless souls who were patients there but I continued to walk to my destination. I was afraid for myself. I didn't know if I would make it out with what little sanity I had left. I could not understand why God would continue to allow these things to happen to me. I had learned to press on through the torment, but the enemy was telling me this was it for me.

As I entered the area where her mother was, I greeted her and could see that she was very ill. Quincianne (Quincy for short) was unable to speak above a whisper. As I touched her hand, I asked if she would mind if I prayed for her. For the space of about five minutes, the angels of God held back the torment from me and the power of God touched her. There was no immediate visible change, but I had an assurance that death would not prevail.

As I left the hospital, I began to shake. The spirits had reattached themselves to me. It felt as if I was being punished for praying for Quincy. I didn't share with Vernita what was happening to me as I didn't want her to feel guilty for asking me to pray for her mother. The next morning, as the nurse entered her mother's room she found her singing. The nurse was shocked because only a few hours before there wasn't much hope. When the nurse inquired about the sudden change, all Quincy could do was give God the glory. Two days later she was released from the hospital, but I continued to suffer.

Chapter Three

Free
At Last

I became a master at hiding my torment from others. It wasn't as difficult in this new state because, for the most part, no one knew who the old Doll was. I knew and my husband knew, but I pretended with him as well. I would find an isolated place to cry. The only thing I enjoyed about my long ride to work was that I could cry and talk to God in privacy.

It always amazed me how the Lord would bless despite my affliction. My mind and memory had suffered so that it was difficult to think. Each time I had to teach a class, or prepare some type of document, the Holy Ghost would step in and somehow do what I couldn't do. My brain cells didn't seem to work correctly. I had to take excessive notes in all meetings because I could never remember what was said. Even when I participated, I could not recall important discussions.

I am grateful for my sons. To this day, they help me recapture the past. I don't recall many events in our lives during the years of the torment. Many times I wished I had videotaped all of the special happenings in their lives. I just can't remember, much but I thank God that they now understand what I went through, and they will spend hours reminiscing for me about some of the good times. They tell me of things they did and of what I did or said. We laugh as they re-enact those precious years. Losing their childhood was, for me, so excruciatingly painful, but (glory to God) I am thankful for their keen memories and willingness to recapture those precious moments for me.

After a short period of time, God gave me favor and I received a promotion. I was grateful but what I wanted and needed most of all was to be free, to have peace. I had no one to talk to but God. Why was I continuing to suffer, when the power of God was working all around me?

The Answer

All divine revelations concerning the end of this torment had ceased. Now, I just hoped that each day would bring some answers to my questions. I struggled with the Father's directive to continue taking the last prescription prescribed to me. I also continued to struggle with the mindset of many Christians that taking any medicines for your nerves was bad. I fought God's voice as He constantly reminded me that our human bodies are not designed to take the kind of beatings the enemy places on our emotions. He prompted me to take care of myself. Even when I obeyed and felt better, I continued to fight condemnation. I never told my husband that I continued to take any medication. After all, I have faith. How foolish we are to override the voice of God and listen to man. God's ways are far above our ways.

I received a book in the mail and, to this day, I'm not sure who sent it to me. The book was a little thick and I knew I would have difficulty concentrating. It seemed interesting, but something kept telling me not to read it. I'm not sure how long it took me just to begin reading. When I did start, I couldn't put it down.

The title of the book was, "He Came To Set The Captives Free," by Dr. Rebecca Brown. I had never heard of her so I was really cautious about reading it. I began to read the warning in the beginning of her book. She writes:

This will be one of the hardest books you have ever tried to read. **SATAN DOES NOT WANT YOU TO READ THIS MATERIAL.**

Dr. Brown describes the book as an exposé on the many ways Satan and his demons are at work in the world today. She describes her personal fight, as well as that of a young woman who God had used Dr. Brown to bring out of the Satanic realm of darkness. Rebecca Brown details how she almost lost her life battling the power of darkness.

I covered myself with the blood of Jesus and read page after page. Something was fighting me and the torment continued, but something else was happening to me. I gradually began to feel alive again. I read page after page, barely stopping to tend to my family. The more I read, the more light was shed on my life, my struggles. It was as if I was reading about myself. No, I'm not a doctor, but the events and the happenings were so familiar.

I read and cried but this time they were not tears of pain and frustration. You see, saints, as I read the book, the shackles were breaking off me with each page. The weights were falling to my side. It had taken seven years to get my answer. By the time I finished the book I was free, totally free from years of torment by Satan. The answer was right there in the book. Honestly, when I had read page twenty of the book, my trial was over. Rebecca had gone to die. She had lived in agonizing pain for months and there was no hope. The pastor of her home church came to visit her and he would not accept the fact that she was dying. The following words are taken from her book on pages 20-21:

> He came (Pastor Pat) and talked with her and told
> her that the Lord had revealed to him that it was not

His will for Rebecca to die. Then he said, "I know this sounds crazy, but I believe the Lord has revealed to me that what is happening to you is that you are being attacked by a group of very powerful witches. Your illness has worsened to this point because of the demonic powers they are sending to you."

I truthfully confess to you that at that moment on page 20, God set me free. The rest of the book gave me more insight on my own life. It was the power of witchcraft that had enslaved me. Remember the man at the conference? The man who said, "I'm a Christian?" Exactly seven long years later, I discovered that man was a messenger from Satan. The assignment of witchcraft was sent to stop me from fulfilling my destiny. My divine destiny.

I was in shock for a few days. I looked for my familiar companion. The torment was gone. My body was weak and my mind was tired but my familiar friend was gone. The light had come on and darkness was exposed. I was free. I didn't know what to do with my freedom. I had been tormented, miserable and sick for so long.

My appetite gradually returned. I ate and ate and ate. No more size seven for me. It was time to buy new clothes. I could not believe how good I was beginning to feel. I was alive again. I could enjoy my life, my marriage, my children and my God. I could talk to God without begging and crying for deliverance. I could drive to work on I-95 and not cry. I could drive in rush-hour-traffic and not be tormented. I could grocery shop and not need to run out of the store. I could look forward to sunrise without expecting my old friend again. I could read my bible and sing about the blood without oppression. I WAS FREE!

I was so cautious initially. I wasn't sure this was going to last, but day after day I would awaken without those powers resting on my head. It had been seven long years through the valley of the shadow of death.

The Lack of Knowledge

It is imperative that I share some necessary tools to help those whom Satan has bound with demonic oppression. The word says in Hosea;

My people are destroyed for a lack of knowledge

Precious saints are not just hurting; they are being destroyed for a lack of knowledge. I remember the old saying, "What you don't know can't hurt you." I beg to differ. What you don't know can kill you. My not knowing to keep the armor of God on was detrimental. My not knowing not to open myself up just because someone said they were a Christian, led me through an abyss. Not only did I not know what was happening to me, the countless number of individuals who offered me advice and counsel, were not enlightened about the destruction of the devil sent against me.

As I have previously shared, I went to two therapists and two psychiatrists for answers. I went to several churches for help, but I was unable to get the key to my problems. I was told to bind the devil, plead the blood of Jesus, march around my house seven times, give to certain ministries, fast, pray, tithe, anoint myself, anoint my children and walk in love. Then, of course, I was presented with the conclusion that there must be some unconfessed sin in my life that had brought such devastation and I must be reaping the things I had sown. The list goes on and on. While many of the instructions were godly things to do, they were not the solution for my deliverance. I walked under so much condemnation for what I was told was my lack of faith. Without faith, I could not have put one foot in front of the other on a daily basis. Without faith, I could not have faced each dreaded day of torment.

Let's turn to the book of Job. Make no mistake; I am not comparing myself to Job. Let's just analyze what Job went through.

The bible describes Job as an upright man who feared God and resisted evil. Satan had his eye on Job. Chapter 1 verses 6-12 details how Satan came before the Lord when the angels of God came to present themselves. God questioned Satan about his activities.

> And the Lord said to Satan, From where did you come?
> Then Satan answered the Lord, From going to and fro
> on the earth and from walking up and down on it.

And the Lord said, Have you considered my servant Job, that there is none like him on the earth. A blameless and upright man; one who reverently fears God, and abstains from and shuns evil because it is wrong.

Satan then goes on to persuade God to remove the hedge of protection He has placed around Job and his family.

I have heard, for many years, the teaching that the things that befell Job were a result of his fears. I wish to offer a revelation from the Holy Ghost through my own trial and experience. In Job chapter 3:25, Job says:

> For the thing which I greatly fear comes upon me, and
> that of which I am afraid befalls me.

When the hedge of protection was taken away from Job he began to feel the activities in the demonic realm. This was foreign to Job because he had walked so faithfully in the presence of God, that God himself described him as a perfect and upright man. When the Lord allows you to feel the uninhibited weapons the enemy is sending against you, there is no way not to feel fear. Fear is the opposite of faith. With God's presence there is faith, with Satan's presence there is fear. The forces of darkness bring pain, heartache and destruction. While Job was not aware that the devil had petitioned the Father for him, he could feel the Satanic presence around him and he could see the devastation.

If a burglar enters your home and you know he's there, but don't know where, would there not be fear? Would you not consider what kind of weapon he might have? Would you not consider that you could possibly die? Now is that fear, wisdom, or just the knowing that something or someone evil is attempting to snatch away what is rightfully yours? When evil is lurking in the dark and God has permitted it, all you can do is go through. If Job had sinned at some point, he would have been able to recognize the reason for the vicious attacks. He had already earned the trust and respect of his Father. Surely, his Father would have revealed his sin to him.

Prior to my separation from my husband, the Lord told me he would be with another woman. That information brought fear. I never uttered my fear. However, because of the ever present darkness, no matter what I prayed it still happened. I was powerless to stop this because it was permitted by God. The Lord said to Satan, all that he has is in your power, but spare his life. When God speaks a word, no one is letting it happen. He gave Satan the go ahead.

I am keenly aware that there are incidences where prayer and supplication changed the mind of God, but don't allow the enemy to cause you to miss the point. Job was in the fire to illustrate God's complete confidence in him. God knew what Job was made of ahead of time. He knew the outcome. He trusted Job. We know Job trusted God by Job's own admission in chapter 13 verse 15:

> *Though he slay me, yet will I trust him, but I will maintain mine own ways before him.*

We recognize that God was not afflicting Job, Satan was. However, "All power belongs to God." Satan could not touch Job without God's permission. Job was in relationship with the Father and he would not let his circumstances turn him around. Another example of this type of commitment was when Jesus hung on the cross. Matthew 27:45-46 reads:

> *Now from the sixth hour there was darkness over all the land unto the ninth hour.*

> *And about the ninth hour Jesus cried with a loud voice, Eli, Eli, lama sabachthini? that is to say, My God, My God, why hast thou forsaken me?*

The key word is "darkness." Webster defines darkness as: 1) absence of light; obscurity; gloom. 2) that quality or state which renders anything difficult to be understood.

For three hours, Jesus was without the presence of his father. During that time, he was not only dealing with the pain of the cross, but with the presence of hosts of darkness without the presence of the Father. That anguish caused him to cry out in pain, "Why have you forsaken me?" When darkness surrounds us, without God there is fear. Moments in the presence of Satanic forces seem like hours. Their evil seems to pull against the force of gravity. Honestly, without the power of God holding you back, humans cannot resist the pull on their own. John 10:10 says:

The thief comes not but to **steal, kill and to destroy**

Webster defines steal: to take without permission or right, secretly or by force. Kill is defined: to cause to die; deprive of life and Destroy is defined: to injure beyond repair of renewal. 2. to put an end to; extinguish. Those who are on Satan's hit list basically have a contract against them with the orders to **steal, kill and destroy** them. There is no witness protection program. Many soldiers have to face their unseen attacker and desperately need God's intercessors to stand for them. Many a soldier in God's army will face severe attack for their willingness to set the captives free. They must grit their teeth, fasten on the armor and fight. Many patriarchs in the bible were ministered to by angels before their battles. They were usually greeted with the same greeting, "Fear not." When faced with a life and death situation, they had to deal with fear.

I am not describing day to day fears (which I believe are sent by the devil as a tool to hinder); I am talking about the oppressive fear that comes from the onslaught of the enemy. I am talking about fighting an unseen force, which is slowly drawing the life from you like a cancer that cannot be detected by any medical device. Such unexplainable events will bring some type of fear.

Imagine, if possible, how Job was feeling. He could not find an area in his life that has caused such destruction. Job knew the teaching of the Bible. Can you imagine the fear and anguish he felt, trying to explain to other men of God that he had done nothing wrong that he knew of? Can you imagine the torment of hearing your friends accuse you of sin that does not exist in your life?

Job's Accusers

Most tragic, to me, is that these friends could not feel the ever present darkness surrounding Job. They were quite aware of the word as it was written, but were unable to recognize the powers of hell present in their midst. Their lack of knowledge inflicted even more torment upon their friend. They were unaware that the devil was using them, as they repeatedly reprimanded Job for sins that were nonexistent in his life. Dear children of God, I am not magnifying the devil. My only desire is to enlighten the eyes of your understanding. Don't ever underestimate the power of your enemy.

My sons play football, and one year they were certain to win their season opener. The team was very confident and the coach told them that the game would be an easy win. Their opponents had played losing seasons for the past few years, so this school had been chosen for the first game in order to build our team's confidence for a winning year. The outcome was disastrous. Their opponents beat them 31-6. The players were devastated. Most of the young men walked to the locker room in tears. I went to comfort some of them and one of our players said, "We were supposed to beat them. They are one of the sorriest teams." I looked that young man in the eye and said, "You underestimated the ability of your opponent? They were not mentally prepared for such a battle. They had been given the wrong information.

After so many years of intense torment, I get easily grieved by the reckless comments and teaching in the Body of Christ. I have listened to many preachers make statements like, "Just show me where the devil is and I'll get him." We act as though we can use God's power anytime we want. Rest assured, if you are walking in the anointing and power of God, or if you are destined for greatness, I guarantee you, Satan knows where you are. You don't have to look for him. Frankly, if you know of someone who is obeying God, watch closely. Satan is close by.

If Job's fear had caused the entire calamity then why does God say in Job 2:3,

And the Lord said to Satan, Have you considered my servant Job, that there is none like him on the earth, a blameless and upright man, one who (reverently) fears God and abstains from and shuns all evil (because it is wrong)? And still he holds fast his integrity, although you move me against him to destroy him **WITHOUT** *cause.*

If fear is what many interpret as the reason for Job's calamity, how do we explain what God himself said? What an atrocity to blame this man that God found no fault in.

Ability vs. Experience

The Lord told me many years ago that ability is no good without experience. We may possess ability to do great things, but without experience we speak and instruct purely from head knowledge.

My friend Shirley does not presently have any children, while I have been wonderfully blessed with three sons. Shirley has not experienced childbirth, so if she were asked to be a birthing coach, she could help by sharing what she has read, seen, or heard. However she cannot identify with the pain the person feels who is in labor. Why? Simply because she has had no experience.

Job's friends could not relate to his anguish because they had studied the Word, but their faith had not been tried in the area in which Job's was being tried. Job's friend Eliphaz said in Job 4:8

As I myself have seen, those who plow iniquity and sow trouble and mischief reap the same.

By the breath of God they perish and by the blast of His anger they are consumed.

Eliphaz spoke of what he had seen; not of what he had experienced. These repeated instructions from his friends increased Job's anguish. His desperation is described in chapter 6:9

> *I even wish that it would please God to crush me, that*
> *he would let loose his hand and cut me off.*

I recall many nights praying for death. Perhaps an understanding ear would have given Job a small ray of hope. Instead of his friends interceding for him until the answer came, he was judged and condemned.

I realize that there is a price to pay for sin and we do reap what we sow. I understand that there are scriptures that apply to those circumstances. However, my instruction from the Father is to expose the works of darkness, especially in the Body of Christ.

Help for the Captives

I will not attempt to give a formula as a sure cure for the oppressed. I will, however, enlighten you on some of the ways to discern when someone is tormented by the devil, especially by the spirit of witchcraft.

Witchcraft is a spirit that attacks the mind and the emotions, as well as the physical body. One of its greatest tools is its effect on the mind and thought process. As my journey with witchcraft began, my reasoning was greatly affected. Witchcraft is a slow time-released process. Its effect is gradual. I suppose it is somewhat like Alzheimer's disease. There are periods of time when it can be difficult to determine what is real and what is not. This spirit challenges the very foundation of the authenticity of God. By affecting the mind, it is easy to get to the emotions. When the mind and emotions are affected, panic is an ongoing state of being. A person under this demonic attack walks in constant uncertainties. They become unsure of who they are, no matter how certain they were before the onset of the attack. As a victim of such an attack, it was easy for the enemy to use childhood scars to intensify the pain in me.

Somehow, witchcraft takes your dreams and visions and gives you a black screen of despair. It heightens your feelings of desperation, or takes away your true feelings altogether. A person strongly affected by this power begins to lose the light in their eyes. The strain of the demonic pressure can be detected by the weary look deep in their eyes. The eyes are the windows of the soul and this power diminishes the brightness and sparkle once present in the person's eyes. It gives the appearance of chronic depression. Laughter ceases and life itself becomes a chore. A person tormented by witchcraft is constantly trying to determine how others can laugh at a joke, enjoy a summer breeze, or even take a leisurely walk in the park. They can no longer feel the enjoyment that special dates and events used to bring.

There is an extreme difference between someone who is tormented by witchcraft and someone operating in witchcraft. I am not describing those who are direct servants of Satan, who have sought him for this power. Those individuals, like Satan, are transformed into angels of light and can only be discerned by the power of God. The distinctions I am referring to are about those who indirectly, and due to their disobedience to the will of God, have opened the door for the enemy to operate in their lives in witchcraft. I repeat, the eyes are the windows to the soul. A person operating in this power has a cold look in their eyes. Sometimes, the look is lifeless and chilling. The individual often appears to be driven. They look as though a power has taken over their body and has put them to sleep. These individuals have oftentimes walked in a strong rebellion against the will of God. I Samuel 15:23 says:

> For rebellion is as the sin of witchcraft, and stubbornness is as iniquity and idolatry.

Just the other day, I was in the office of a co-worker. As I was talking to him, I could suddenly feel the strong presence of a demonic spirit. This person knows the gift that God has given me and as we talked I said, "I feel witchcraft." I was not implying that it was on him. In fact, I gave assurances that it was not him. We continued to discuss the business at hand, but the power of darkness was strong all around me. After briefly meeting with another staff member, I went back to my office. As soon as I sat behind my desk, a person who had previously worked for the company, walked by my office. This person, who professes Christianity, operates in deliberate rebellion to any of the Word she doesn't agree with. When I checked with another worker, this woman had entered the building at the exact time I had said that I felt witchcraft. When she left, it left. When demonic activity is around and you cannot isolate it to a particular person or thing, there is an uneasiness that resembles fear.

Direct rebellion against the will of God opens the door to witchcraft and this spirit operates in the church today. Many pastors come under direct attack from the power of witchcraft from their members who will not submit to the Word. As church members continue to justify behaviors which are in direct opposition to the Word of God, their resistance gives the devil authority to begin his process of destruction. Satan is crafty, but once he uses us he discards us as useless garbage.

While no one had the answer for me, one of the wisest individuals of all throughout my torment was my cousin Laura. Laura's phone call while I was in the hospital brought insight even though she had no solution. She told me the Lord had revealed to her in prayer that the battle was a spiritual one. She openly admitted that she didn't understand, and assured me she would stand in the gap for me.

The numerous times I spoke with Laura throughout those years of torment she never once attempted to give me her opinion. She listened as I shared with her what was happening to me. She never made any suggestions on what I should do. I could tell she was hurting for me. However, she didn't add to the torment. She recognized her limitations as she provided the needed listening ear. At the end of each visit or conversation she would say, "Honey, I'm praying for you." She would assure me that she believed God for my deliverance. Although she didn't give me any answers to my problem, she didn't pass judgment, criticize, or tell me what she thought was wrong. She did the most important thing that she could; she prayed. As I think of her I can hear the words of the song; <u>Somebody prayed for me</u>:

(Italicized)

> My cousin prayed for me, she had me on her mind,
> she took the time and prayed for me. I'm so glad she
> prayed, I'm so glad she prayed, I'm so glad she prayed
> for me.

Oh, if Job's friends would have just prayed for him.

Sister Jacque was my strongest support. I always found comfort in knowing that she didn't believe I was crazy. She stood in prayer and encouraged me to do the things that the demons were telling me I couldn't do. She was able to give me support because she, too, had experienced years of unexplainable torment. She often described to me a power that would make her feel so afraid, that at one point, her husband had to come home from work to pray for her. She said the power was (as she put it) "trying to take her out." Sister Jacque grew up in Denver, Colorado and, prior to her salvation, was well acquainted with pimps, prostitutes and drug dealers. She did not scare easily, but this unseen force could not be detected even by her husband, who was a man of God, and it was trying to drive her totally insane.

Sister Jacque provided help without enabling me. She encouraged me to take the medicine that was giving me the most help. She knew that it would be unwise to share with anyone else the need to take the medication and she knew how condemned I felt for taking anything. Jacque would always say, "Sister Doll, they don't understand."

One Sunday morning, one of the saints had called her with an urgent message that I was about to commit suicide. Actually I wasn't, but I suppose that as I described what was happening to me at that particular time, they believed that I was going to end my life. Around 8:00 a.m. someone was beating on my door. When I opened it, there stood Jacque in a trench coat, slippers and pajamas. She hadn't stopped to call, she just immediately left her family and her obligation to be at church on time, to come to my aid.

More than anything the tormented person needs someone to commit themselves to be an intercessor. Someone who will stand in the gap and is willing to take a few punches from the devil because they dared to interfere with his plan. James 5:16 says:

> *The effectual fervent prayer of a righteous man availeth much.*

Ephesians 6:18 reads: "Praying always with all prayer and supplication in the Spirit, and watching thereunto with all perseverance and supplication for all saints." Supplication is defined as an entreating, continued, strong, and incessant pleading until prayer is answered. It takes a committed person to endure with incessant pleading when there is no answer in sight for a long period of time. Often, we give up when we don't see results. God wants his servants to develop endurance, for endurance is not only for the person who is being tried, but also for those who are committed to praying until the answer comes. Webster defines endurance as the fact or power of enduring or bearing **anything**. 2) lasting quality. To endure is: to hold out against, to sustain or undergo without impairment or yielding; 2) to bear without resistance or with patience; tolerate. If we are to effectively walk in the love of God we must develop endurance. II Corinthians 13:4 reads:

> Love **endures** long and is patient and kind.

How long were Job's friends in his presence before they became frustrated, judgmental, self righteous and critical? How long did they endure before they offered their opinions and solutions? Job could have benefited from the love of his friends, but he received judgment instead. Job's friend Zophar states in Job 11:13-15

> If you set your heart aright and stretch out your hands to God;

> If you put sin out of your hand and far away from you and let not evil dwell in your tents

> Then can you lift up your face to Him without stain of sin (and unashamed) yes, you shall be steadfast and secure; you shall not fear.

Job answered in Chapter 12:2:

> No doubt you are the (only wise) people (in the world), and wisdom will die with you! Amplified

I can't emphasize enough the damage inflicted by our lack of wisdom, knowledge, and experience. So often, when someone we know battles with cancer or some other debilitating condition, there are people there to comfort, encourage and support them during those battles. You hear others tell the afflicted one how strong, courageous and brave they are for the tenacity displayed during this vicious attack. However, those who the enemy fights in their mind and/or emotions often suffer alone and are viewed as weak. What a shame that we categorize Satan's attacks and rank them. Any attack that severely alters one's ability to function in the perfection that the Father ordained for them, is a Satanic assignment which must not be rated and ranked according to what the "world" views as acceptable or tragic. The Body of Christ must be able to discern **"all"** Satanic attacks and to deal with them as such without wavering and compromising their compassion for the oppressed. Seek God before you offer any suggestions as solutions, or pass judgment on another person's deliverance or the lack thereof.

Finally My Brethren

My desire for the spiritual gift of discerning of spirits did not come without a price. To whom much is given, much is required. I did not know what would be required of me because of that request. I had no idea I would go through the valley of the shadow of death. I did not know that I would be on Satan's hit list. Neither did I realize, nor remotely think, that there would be an assignment, a contract out on me. I didn't know I would be tried by fire to see if God could trust me with this precious gift.

I realize that in the beginning Satan took advantage of my naiveté. My lack of knowledge of him and his craftiness was one of his greatest weapons. Satan took advantage of my lack of ability to recognize him. I had learned scriptures, becoming proficient in quoting quite a bit of the Word. I had learned "church" as I had much exposure to many forms of worship. I had even learned a little about what I would call "fake anointing."

Early in my walk with the Lord, I had visited a church with some friends of mine. This particular church had an evangelist who often ministered from the pulpit. On one occasion, I went to the altar for prayer and this particular evangelist laid his hand on my head and began to pray for me. As he prayed, he attempted to push me down. Everyone else before me had been "Slain in the spirit." As he tried to push me down, I resisted and he told me, "The Lord wants you to yield."

I replied, "I have yielded!" and I refused to fall. He was not going to get the glory, because I knew it was not God.

I know that the angels of God encamp around about us. I also now know that the demons of darkness lurk close by and report back our activities to their master. I realize that the pastor who molested me was simply a tool to damage me at an early age, for the devil knew he could use that at a later date. The key, however, is I know that now. I didn't know it then.

The devil knew that I had a trusting nature and he recognized my desire to please God. He strategized against me early in my life, because he knew he might need a trump card that he could play at a later date to stop God's plan. He gambled on my lack of knowledge of certain scriptures. One scripture in particular, which I knew in my head, needed to be applied in my daily living. I John 4:1-3 tells us:

> Beloved, DO not put faith in every spirit, but prove (test) the spirits to discover whether they proceed from God: for many false prophets have gone forth into the world.

> By this may you know (perceive and recognize) the Spirit of God: every spirit which acknowledges and

confesses (the fact) that Jesus Christ (the Messiah) (actually) has become man and has come in the flesh is of God (has God for its source.)

And every spirit which does not acknowledge and confess that Jesus Christ has come in the flesh (but would annul, destroy, sever, disunite Him) is not of God (does not proceed from him). This (nonconfession) is the (spirit) of the Antichrist, (of) which you heard that it was coming, and now it is already in the world.
Amplified

Satan sent an assassin to the conference, who simply said to me, "I am a Christian." I gave him my full attention and opened myself up "spiritually" to him. He never mentioned Jesus being Lord, or the Son of God. He only said he was a Christian and I gave him my **UNDIVIDED** attention. Besides that, he looked kind and harmless. What a tragic mistake. I was so excited about the conference that I made a critical and foolish mistake. I was so captivated by the potentials of my future that I overrode scriptural principles. Dear friends, nothing that is going to happen tomorrow takes precedence over the important occurrences of today. How often do we neglect our friends, loved ones, and businesses, which need our attention today, by focusing on things of tomorrow? I allowed my excitement for what could be, to override the principle in Matthew 12:33:

For the tree is known by his fruit

I mistook a kind and gentle voice as fruit. I did not know that man well enough to know if he had any fruit. I looked on the outside (which appeared safe) and simply gave him the trust that had not been earned.

I can truthfully say that I am grateful for my years of suffering, because I learned obedience through the things that I suffered. I have a compassion and a commitment to expose the tools of the devil. God uses me to help wounded and tormented men, women, and children. Often, people who are experiencing vicious attacks, severe mind battles and other cruel satanic powers fighting against them, look at me and find hope. Honestly, I look at me and find hope. I am so grateful to be clothed and in my right mind.

My process of restoration was very gradual. My mind did not function properly for some time. While the assignment had ended, my healing process came in stages. God began the restoration of the mental faculties I had lost during those seven years. Job's restoration was also gradual. Although, God eventually restored all to him, it was over a period of time. His restoration process must have taken nine to ten years, as evidenced by the ten children he fathered after his trial. Since a normal pregnancy lasts nine months, so it is safe to assume his restoration took a few years, but God is faithful and he promises:

> And I will restore or replace for you the years that the locust has eaten—the hopping locust, the stripping locust, and the crawling locust, My great army which I sent against you. Joel 2:25 (Amplified)

Isaiah 61:7 assures us:

> Instead of your (former) shame you shall have a twofold recompense; instead of dishonor and reproach

(your people) shall rejoice in their portion. Therefore in their land they shall possess double (what they had forfeited): everlasting joy shall be theirs. Amplified

I am blessed to share with you my trials and triumph. It has been a privilege to expose the works of Satan and the Power of God. The enemy fought me tooth and nail in writing this book. With so many roadblocks and hindrances, this effort was almost impossible. I thank God for my faithful intercessors who battled the gates of hell for me so I could complete **"MY ASSIGNMENT"** to help set the captives free.

I thank God for my time of healing. After about one year, the Father graciously took me through another five years of testing and triumph (which I prefer to call my process) as I will share in my next book, "One More River To Cross."

It is a privilege to suffer for the sake of the call. If I suffer with him, I will reign with him. The suffering of this time is not worthy to be compared to the glory which shall be revealed.

I pray, right now, that the eyes of your understanding will be enlightened. I pray for the oppressed and the captives to be loosed from satanic oppression. I plead the blood of Jesus over the tormented and confused minds, and I rebuke and destroy every assignment of the enemy against you and your loved ones in the Name of Jesus. I pray for deliverance, restoration, and healing in the Name of Jesus. Satan, the BLOOD OF JESUS IS AGAINST YOU! To God be the Glory.

With A Made-Up Mind

Helen

About the Author

Helen L. Swift is the founder and pastor of the House of Refuge in Newark, DE. She has a word from the Lord for all who face inexplicable attacks from the enemy. She understands when the x-rays are negative but the pain is real; when the voices of a crowd are clear, but there is no one there but you; when your friends and loved ones say you've lost your mind, but you know you're not crazy, and the simple things you once did with ease now seem insurmountable. God has brought this vessel out of trials that most would have been defeated by. Helen has fought the fight of faith against the unseen forces of darkness. She has battled satanic forces for many years and there is no end in sight. She has accepted the call as another general at war for the sake of the Gospel. This testimony is given so that the captives might know, with blessed assurance, that Jesus has the same miracle-working power today.

To all who need truth, deliverance, healing, understanding and hope, the God of all Grace has sent this one for you.

Order Form

Postal orders:
House of Refuge, P.O. Box 7833, Newark, DE, 19714

Telephone orders: (888) 402-6085

Please send *The Assignment* **to:**

Name: _____

Address: _____

City: _____ State: _____

Zip: _____

Telephone: (_____) _____

Book Price: $10.00

Shipping: $3.00 for the first book and $1.00 for each additional book to cover shipping and handling withing US, Canada, and Mexico. International orders add $6.00 for the first book and $2.00 for each additional book

Or order from:
Books, Etc.
PO Box 4888
Seattle, WA 98104

(800) 917-BOOK